DOKKÔDÔ

THE 7-DAY RESET

Miyamoto Musashi's 21 Principles
to Build Self-Discipline, Clear Judgment
and Strength Under Pressure

Source and Interpretation Notice
This book is an original contemporary work inspired by the principles of Miyamoto Musashi and *Dokkōdō* (*The Way of Walking Alone*). It is not intended to serve as a definitive academic translation, critical edition, or historical text, but as a practical interpretation for modern readers.

Illustration and Example Notice
Examples, reflections, and scenarios included in this book are used for teaching and illustration. Some details may be adapted, combined, or generalized.

For permissions, bulk sales, or special inquiries, contact:
Support@ProfessionalSkillsPublishing.com

CONTENTS

Walking Alone in a Crowded World

You picked up this book because it is too loud.

You are living in an era of unprecedented, inescapable noise. Every single day, from the moment your alarm pulls you out of sleep to the second you finally shut your eyes, you are bombarded by a relentless stream of demands, notifications, comparisons, and algorithmic outrage.

Your inbox is a leaky boat you can never quite bail out, constantly filling with other people's manufactured emergencies. Your calendar is dictated by the priorities of everyone but yourself. You are constantly connected, constantly reachable, and completely, deeply exhausted in a way that a weekend of sleep can no longer fix.

You feel like you are playing defense with your own life. You are a reactionary creature, bouncing from one crisis to the next, putting out fires, and hoping that *someday* things will finally slow down enough for you to catch your breath and build the life you actually intended to live.

When the modern world makes us feel this overwhelmed, we naturally look for a way out. We look for a cure. And the multi-billion-dollar self-improvement industry is more than happy to sell us the fantasy of the "perfect routine." They tell us that if we just wake up at 4:00 AM, take a freezing ice bath, drink a perfectly formulated, expensive greens supplement, and stare at a red-light therapy panel while journaling our gratitude, we will finally become disciplined, unshakeable titans.

Or, conversely, they sell us the fantasy of the "escape." They tell us we need to book a remote cabin in the woods, delete all our apps, or attend a $3,000 silent retreat in the mountains to finally find our center and heal our burnout.

But both of these solutions are fragile, highly monetized illusions.

The hyper-optimized, twelve-step morning routine is aesthetic discipline, not functional discipline. It shatters into a million pieces the minute your toddler wakes up sick, your dog throws up on the rug, or your boss calls you at 6:00 AM with a crisis. And the weekend retreat? It's just a temporary geographical cure.

If your mind is a chaotic, resentful storm, you simply pack up the storm in a suitcase and bring it to the quiet cabin with you. You sit in the woods, still obsessing over your inbox. When Monday morning hits, the noise returns, the friction resumes, and you are right back where you started, feeling even worse because the "cure" didn't work.

You cannot buy your way out of the chaos. You cannot retreat from your life to fix your life. You cannot wait for the world to stop being demanding. You need an operating system that works *inside* the mud, the friction, the sticky mess, and the unpredictability of the real world.

You need the *Dokkōdō*.

The Origins of the 21 Precepts

In 1643, Miyamoto Musashi, arguably the most famous, undefeated, and lethal samurai in Japanese history, knew his life was rapidly coming to an end. After surviving over sixty life-or-death duels and navigating the brutal, shifting, and treacherous politics of 17th-century Japan, his legendary body was failing him. Historians believe he was suffering from painful thoracic cancer.

He did not seek out a comfortable feather bed, a host of healers, or a grand audience to fight his inevitable decline. Instead, he stripped away everything. He retreated to the Reigandō (□□□), a damp, isolated, stone "Spirit Rock" cave situated on Mount Iwato, overlooking the sea. He went there to completely eliminate the noise of society and distill everything he had learned about survival, strategy, human weakness, and the mind into ink.

In the final week of his life in 1645, knowing the clock was about to run out, Musashi gave away his remaining worldly possessions to his closest disciples. He then took up his brush and wrote a final, stark document consisting of exactly 21 short, uncompromising rules.

He called it the *Dokkōdō*, which translates roughly to "The Way of Walking Alone."

The *Dokkōdō* is not a martial arts manual. It will not teach you how to swing a katana or win a bar fight. It is an operating system for the human mind. It is a highly concentrated, brutally honest framework for achieving absolute internal sovereignty.

Musashi wrote these 21 precepts to ensure that even as his physical world shrank to the size of a cold stone cave, and even as his body decayed, his mind remained sharp, unburdened by regret, free from the desperate desire for comfort, and completely detached from the fragile ego. He wrote it to be environmentally bulletproof.

Why You Need It Today

We are no longer fighting duels with steel swords to the death. The stakes of our daily lives rarely involve physical bloodshed. But make no mistake: you are in a daily, high-stakes battle for your attention, your agency, and your character.

The modern enemies of discipline are not physical adversaries standing across a field; they are psychological, and they live inside your house. Our modern enemies are the endless pursuit of cheap dopamine to numb our anxiety. They are the paralyzing, suffocating fear of what other people think of us. They are the toxic, energy-draining habit of complaining about our circumstances. And they are the profound, terrifying inability to just sit quietly in a room with our own thoughts without reaching for a screen.

When Musashi talks about "Walking Alone," he is not telling you to abandon your family, quit your job, move to the mountains, and build a physical cave. Solitude, in the modern context, is not physical isolation. "Walking Alone" is a metaphor for internal gravity.

To walk alone means that your focus, your mood, and your daily execution are completely independent of your external environment. It means you do not outsource your emotional regulation to the people around you. You do not need your spouse to be in a perfect mood in order for you to remain calm.

You do not need the office to be completely quiet in order to concentrate and do deep work. You do not need people to praise you and stroke your ego in order to do the right thing. You do not need the weather, the economy, or the traffic to be perfect in order to hold the line.

You carry your own weather. You are your own cave.

The 7-Day Reigandō Reset

This book is not a dry, academic historical analysis of Miyamoto Musashi. It is not a romanticized history lesson about the samurai. It is a highly tactical, unglamorous, modern application of his final words.

Over the next seven days, we are going to use the 21 precepts of the *Dokkōdō* to completely rewire how you respond to stress, friction, and your own ego.

We have divided the 21 rules into seven distinct days, tackling three precepts per day. You will not be practicing these rules in a vacuum or on a vacation. This is a live-fire exercise. You will be practicing them in the middle of your daily commute, in your chaotic kitchen while making dinner, and at your stressful office during meetings that could have been emails.

Because direct advice often triggers our ego's defenses, this book shows you exactly how this integration works by following two avatars, Nate and Cole, as they navigate this exact 7-day retreat. They represent the two most common ways modern people fail at discipline.

Nate is the avatar of "Soft Chaos"; he is an overwhelmed, distracted father with an unpredictable schedule who constantly succumbs to comfort and the path of least resistance.

Cole is the avatar of "Brittle Iron"; he is a rigid, divorced executive who uses extreme, punishing structure and fitness as emotional armor to avoid vulnerability, making him highly prone to anger when his routines are broken.

Through their stories, you will see exactly how Musashi's ancient rules apply to spilled oatmeal, failed business pitches, toxic coworkers, broken workout routines, and deeply strained relationships. You will see your own excuses mirrored in their struggles.

Here is what this 7-day retreat is designed to accomplish:

1. **Destroy the Victim Narrative:** You will learn to stop actively arguing with reality and step into the mud. You will recognize how much vital energy you waste wishing things were different, and you will learn to immediately accept the board state and handle the friction without a single complaint.

2. **Sever the Tie Between Mood and Action:** You will learn how to fully recognize and feel your emotions without letting them dictate your behavior. You will learn how to

execute your intentions when you are exhausted, angry, or unmotivated.

3. **Shrink the Ego and Detach:** You will learn the difference between apathy and true detachment. You will learn how to care deeply and passionately about your effort, while radically detaching from the final outcome, freeing yourself from the fear of failure and the desperate need for external validation.

4. **Master the Return:** Most importantly, you will unlearn the toxic myth of the "perfect streak." You will learn the true definition of discipline. Discipline is not an unbroken record of perfection. Discipline is simply the speed at which you return to your standard immediately after you inevitably fail.

You are holding a 400-year-old blueprint for mental survival. The noise of the modern world is not going away. The world is not going to suddenly slow down, apologize, and wait for you to catch up.

It is time to stop looking for a comfortable escape. It is time to build the fortress inside yourself. Turn the page to Day 0, and let's set your cave.

DAY 0:

THE SETUP NIGHT

T he cave wasn't magic. It was just quiet.

When Miyamoto Musashi retired to the Reigandō cave in 1645 to write his final works, including the 21 precepts of the *Dokkōdō*, he wasn't trying to become a mystic. He wasn't looking to transcend his humanity, achieve an elevated state of esoteric consciousness, or unlock a secret meditation hack to sell to the masses.

He was an aging warrior at the absolute end of a violent, chaotic life. His body was actively failing him, riddled with what historians believe was thoracic cancer.

He walked into that cave to simply strip away the noise. He was documenting a way of walking through the world that relied entirely on internal gravity, rather than external validation, the endless pursuit of comfort, or the comforting delusions of society. He wrote the rules to ensure his mind remained sharp, infinitely adaptable, and fundamentally unburdened, even as his physical world rapidly shrank to the size of a stone room.

You do not have a cave. In fact, you live in the exact opposite of a cave. You live in the Anti-Cave.

You have a mortgage that demands a massive portion of your labor every thirty days. You have an inbox that refills like a leaky boat in a storm, requiring you to frantically bail water before you have even poured your morning coffee. You have complex relationships that require constant, careful, and often exhausting emotional maintenance.

Most dangerously, you have an attention span that has been ruthlessly weaponized against you by billion-dollar algorithms explicitly designed by behavioral psychologists to keep you scrolling, outraged, and consuming.

You probably have a low-grade, persistent hum of anxiety in the back of your mind, a quiet but incredibly steady voice telling you that you are somehow falling behind your peers, failing your potential, or running out of time to figure it all out.

Most modern productivity and wellness advice tells you that to fix this overwhelming sensation, you need to escape. You need to buy your way out of the chaos with luxury. You need to book a weekend cabin getaway, attend a $3,000 silent retreat in the mountains, or build a perfectly optimized, aesthetically pleasing morning routine that requires waking up at 3:30 AM, drinking perfectly balanced alkaline water, and taking a plunging ice bath before the sun even breaches the horizon.

But you cannot retreat from your life to fix your life. The "geographical cure" is a lie; if your mind is a storm, you will simply bring the storm to the quiet cabin. You have to build the retreat *inside* your existing life. You have to learn how to find absolute, unshakeable stillness in the fluorescent-lit grocery store aisle. You must learn to maintain your focus in the middle of a chaotic, open-office floor plan while a coworker talks loudly on speakerphone. You must summon deep, grounded patience when your kid is screaming in the backseat of the car during gridlocked, bumper-to-bumper rush hour traffic.

Welcome to the Reigandō Reset.

Over the next seven days, we are going to use Musashi's 21 rules to build a highly functional, entirely repeatable operating system for calm discipline. There will be no samurai cosplay here.

We are not going to pretend you don't care about your family, your career trajectory, or your electric bill. Detachment does not mean emotional numbness, and solitude does not mean isolating yourself from the people who rely on you for their survival.

This is about building a specific, highly resilient kind of anchored strength, the kind of ugly, unglamorous, deeply practical strength that works when the baby is sick, the client is furious, or the alarm goes off and the house is freezing cold.

To do this, we are going to follow two men walking the exact same seven-day retreat, using two completely different schedules.

Because there is no "perfect" way to do this. There is only the way that works for the raw, unedited, messy life you actually have.

Meet the Paths

Nate (The Flexible Path)

Nate is 34. He is a Product Manager at a mid-sized tech company. He has a wife, Claire, a three-year-old son, a five-year-old daughter, and a hybrid-remote job that constantly bleeds into his evenings, blurring the lines between his living room and his boardroom until he never feels like he is truly "off the clock."

His Baseline: Nate is completely, deeply exhausted in a way that a full eight hours of sleep doesn't seem to fix. He operates entirely on defensive reaction. His day rarely belongs to him. He wakes up to a toddler standing on his chest, instantly checks Slack through one open eye to see what fires started overseas overnight, and spends his entire day toggling frantically between urgent emails, unfinished projects, and household chores, never once feeling like he's actually caught up.

He is a good man who genuinely loves his family, but he is constantly distracted. Last week, he nodded along to a story his daughter was telling him while secretly drafting an email in his head; he couldn't remember a single word she said. He is desperately seeking the approval of his bosses and using cheap comfort to cope with his chronic stress.

By 9:30 PM, when the kids are finally asleep and the house is blessedly quiet, the exact moment he *could* be doing the deep, focused work to better himself, he doesn't read, stretch, or meditate. He collapses.

He doomscrolls on the couch, the artificial blue light washing over his tired face, and eats stale cereal in the dark kitchen because he feels he is fundamentally "owed" some mindless dopamine after surviving the gauntlet of another day.

Nate desperately wants discipline, but he believes a toxic internet myth: he thinks true discipline requires unbroken silence, perfect aesthetics, and total, authoritarian control over his calendar. Because his life is inherently chaotic, sticky, and loud, he assumes he is permanently disqualified from being a disciplined man.

He thinks he needs the cave, and since he doesn't have it, he defaults to the chaos, letting the current drag him wherever it wants.

Cole (The Structured Path)

Cole is 46. He is an Operations Director for a regional supply firm. He is divorced and shares custody of his two teenage kids, Jackson and Chloe. He spent four years in military logistics before transitioning to the corporate world, and he brought the heavy regimentation with him into civilian life.

His Baseline: Cole is unyieldingly rigid. He wakes up at 4:30 AM every single day, without fail, regardless of how he slept. He works out in his freezing, stripped-down garage gym, lifting heavy iron in the dark to the smell of old rubber stall mats and climbing chalk.

He eats the exact same macro-counted meals out of glass containers, wears the same dark colors to minimize decision fatigue, and runs his entire life on a meticulously color-coded spreadsheet. On paper, and to his intimidated coworkers, Cole is the absolute, unquestionable picture of dominant discipline.

But Cole's discipline is actually a form of armor. He uses his rigorous, punishing structure to actively avoid dealing with reality. He uses his schedule to avoid the undeniable fact that his house feels incredibly empty since the divorce, his relationship with his teenage son is dangerously strained, and he fundamentally doesn't know how to just *sit still* without feeling utterly useless, highly anxious, and vulnerable.

He takes immense pride in his toughness and his ability to endure physical pain, but his emotional rigidity makes him incredibly brittle. When his son changes weekend plans at the last minute, Cole doesn't adapt gracefully, his frustration flashes into a quiet, intimidating anger that sucks all the oxygen out of the room.

He is physically present, but emotionally walled off behind a fortress of routine. While Nate uses comfort to cope with his lack of control, Cole is using total, unyielding control to cope with his profound fear of vulnerability and failure.

The Two Tracks

Over the next seven days, Nate and Cole will confront the exact same three daily precepts. But their daily schedules, and the specific way they are forced to implement these rules, will look entirely different. You must choose one of their tracks for your own retreat.

Track A: Nate's Flexible Retreat (Anchored Blocks)

Best for: Parents of young kids, shift workers, first responders, and people whose days are highly unpredictable by necessity.

You cannot control your timeline, so we will not waste vital energy trying. Fighting a chaotic, reactive schedule with a rigid, color-coded spreadsheet only leads to immediate failure, deep frustration, and self-loathing. Instead of fixed hours, Track A relies on **Three Daily Anchors**.

An anchor is not a tether; it is a heavy weight that keeps you from drifting entirely out to sea when the storm hits. You hit these anchors whenever the windows of time naturally open. If you get interrupted halfway through an anchor by a crying child, an urgent phone call, or a sudden crisis, you do not panic.

You pause, handle the chaos with a level head, and then return to the anchor. The discipline is in the *return*, not the unbroken perfection of the execution.

1. **Morning Anchor (10-25 min):** Read the daily precepts + execute the morning practice. You do this whenever the very first window opens. Maybe it's sitting in the dark kitchen before the house wakes up, maybe it's sitting in your parked car for ten minutes before walking into the office, or maybe it's on the train commute.

2. **Midday Anchor (5-15 min):** A tactical reset drill. This is explicitly designed to sever the momentum of a stressful day. It acts as a psychological circuit breaker to prevent you from carrying morning frustrations, a bad meeting, or an argument into your afternoon workflow or evening family time.

3. **Evening Anchor (10-25 min):** Journaling the daily prompts + writing out tomorrow's "Carry Card." You do this when the dust finally settles, actively processing the day before you allow yourself to check out, scroll social media, or sleep for the night. This closes the psychological loop of the day.

Track B: Cole's Structured Retreat (Fixed Schedule)

Best for: Empty-nesters, single professionals, or anyone with high autonomy over their calendar who thrives on exactness and desperately needs a hard reset to break out of a comfortable rut.

If you want to test your ability to hold a hard, uncompromising line, and if your life actually allows for it without neglecting your dependents, this is your track. You will lock in exact times for your retreat requirements on Setup Night, and you will defend those blocks ruthlessly against your own excuses, fatigue, and the casual demands of others.

- **0500 – Wake & Silence Walk:** 15 minutes of moving outside immediately after waking up. No inputs allowed. No phone, no music, no podcasts, no checking email. Just you, the morning air, and your own unedited, raw thoughts.

- **0600 – Reading Block:** Study the daily precepts with a pen in hand. Annotate what challenges you.

- **0630 – Practice Block:** Execute the morning physical or mental drill with total, unbroken focus.

- **0800 to 1700 – Work/Training:** The uncompromising, distraction-free execution of your daily professional or personal duties. You do not check social media. You do not gossip. You execute.

- **1200 – Midday Reset:** A strict 10-minute disconnection block. You stop working, physically step away from the screen, leave your phone behind, and intentionally reset your posture and mind.

- **2000 – Evening Reflection:** Journaling the daily prompts + writing out tomorrow's "Carry Card." Once this is done, the day is officially sealed and closed. You do not reopen work emails.

Make Your Decision

Take a moment right now. Look at your life. Choose Nate's flexible track or Cole's structured track.

This is the very first true test of your honesty on this retreat. **Do not choose the track you *wish* you had the life for.** Ego will try to trick you here, whispering sweet lies about your capacity. Ego will tell the exhausted, sleep-deprived father of a newborn to pick Cole's track to "prove" he's a hardcore warrior, practically guaranteeing a spectacular, self-destructive failure by Wednesday. Ego will tell the single, childless executive with total calendar control to pick Nate's track because she "just wants to go with the flow" and avoid holding herself accountable to a hard standard.

Choose the track that fits the raw, unedited, messy reality of your calendar tomorrow morning.

If your life is highly unpredictable, do not choose Cole's track; you are setting yourself up for guaranteed failure, which will just give your brain a highly convenient excuse to quit the retreat entirely by Day 2. Choose Nate's track and do the grueling, highly unglamorous hard work of learning how to be disciplined *inside* the noise.

If you have totally free evenings and a predictable morning, don't hide behind Nate's flexibility to give yourself an easy out. Choose Cole's track, draw a hard line in the sand, and hold your feet to the fire.

Either way, the retreat works. The rules do not care about your timeline, your aesthetics, or your excuses. They only care about your execution.

Setup Night: Set Your Cave

The retreat begins tomorrow morning, but your success or failure will be decided tonight. Willpower is lowest in the morning; do not rely on it. Before your head hits the pillow tonight, you must do these three things:

1. **Commit to the Track:** Get a physical piece of paper. Write down "Track A" or "Track B." Put it on your nightstand or tape it directly to your bathroom mirror. Make the decision real, physical, and highly visible.

2. **Remove the Friction:** Do not waste cognitive energy on logistics at 6:00 AM when your brain is foggy.

   ○ *If you chose Track A:* Decide exactly *where* your morning anchor will happen so you aren't sleepily wandering around the house looking for a quiet spot while your motivation drains.

   ○ *If you chose Track B:* Set your alarm, lay out your clothes, and physically place your phone in another room so you cannot blindly reach it from the bed and start scrolling.

3. **Clear the Deck:** Look at your calendar for the next seven days. Find one thing, a meeting you don't really need to attend, a social obligation you only agreed to out of guilt or fear of missing out, or an hour of television you watch out of pure habit, and cancel it. Buy yourself back one hour of margin for this week. You are going to need the space to breathe and process.

Tomorrow morning, you face Precepts 1 through 3. The time for wishing for a different schedule, a different life, or a different set of circumstances is completely over. Tomorrow, we stop arguing with reality and start working with it.

Set your environment. Clear your mind. Get some sleep.

DAY 1:

REALITY, NOT FANTASY

The single greatest source of modern anxiety is the massive, yawning gap between reality and fantasy, between how things actually, physically are in the present moment, and how we stubbornly, desperately demand they "should" be.

We suffer because we believe life owes us a frictionless experience. When you step into Day 1, the very first thing your brain will do is complain about the specific conditions of the battlefield. It will search desperately for any excuse to delay the work.

You will think, *I didn't get enough sleep to start a retreat today. I feel groggy. The house is too loud. My boss sent a highly stressful email at 6:00 AM, so my focus is shot and today is officially ruined. I will start tomorrow when things are perfectly aligned.*

Musashi did not demand perfect weather, a fully rested body, a full stomach, or ideal footing before drawing his sword. He fought in the thick, clinging mud, on uneven, treacherous ground, often with the blinding sun directly in his eyes. He understood that reality does not negotiate.

Today, we are going to look directly at the mud of our own lives. We are going to intentionally stop fighting the reality of our circumstances and start operating inside them. We are going to address the primary, sneaky ways we try to escape the friction of the present moment, through the constant pursuit of cheap, numbing comfort, and by letting our fleeting, biological moods dictate our permanent actions.

Track A: Nate's Morning

Nate's alarm buzzed at 5:45 AM.

He had meticulously planned his very first Morning Anchor on Setup Night. The vision was highly aesthetic and incredibly satisfying in his mind: he was going to brew an expensive, single-origin pour-over coffee, sit on his back porch wrapped in a blanket while the neighborhood was still draped in quiet darkness, and read the first three precepts of the retreat in profound, unbroken silence. He was finally going to be a disciplined man, just like the hyper-optimized productivity gurus he enviously followed online.

Reality had a vastly different, far messier plan.

At 5:48 AM, just as he was putting his feet on the floor, the door to his bedroom clicked open. His five-year-old daughter, Maya, stood in the hallway holding a stuffed rabbit, looking incredibly pale and frightened. "Dad," she whispered, her voice trembling. "I threw up in my bed."

Nate felt a hot, sickening spike of cortisol hit the back of his neck. *Are you kidding me?* his brain screamed, immediately launching into a well-worn, comfortable victim narrative. *Today? The one day I actually commit to doing something for myself, to getting my life on track, to doing this retreat, and this happens? This shouldn't be happening to me. This isn't fair. The universe is literally working against my discipline.*

He threw off the covers with a heavy sigh. The next forty-five minutes were a blur of exhausting, deeply unglamorous chaos, stripping wet, sour-smelling sheets, running a warm bath, comforting a crying child who was afraid she was in trouble, and starting a load of laundry while trying desperately not to wake the toddler sleeping in the next room. By 6:40 AM, Maya was sitting on the couch wrapped in a towel, watching a cartoon, quietly sipping water. Nate's wife, Claire, emerged from the bedroom, bleary-eyed and exhausted, to take over the morning shift so Nate could get ready for work.

Nate walked into the kitchen and leaned heavily against the cold granite counter. He felt completely defeated before the sun had even fully risen. The aesthetic, perfect morning was dead. His mood was plummeting rapidly into a deep, dark well of self-pity and simmering resentment. He felt like he had already failed the retreat on Day 1.

His hand instinctively reached into his pocket for his phone. He desperately wanted to open Instagram. He wanted to look at other people's perfect, quiet, sun-drenched mornings. He wanted a quick, ten-second hit of algorithmic dopamine to numb the sharp sting of his ruined plan. He wanted the warm, familiar comfort of total digital distraction to take him away from the smell of bleach and the exhaustion in his bones.

He pulled the phone out. His thumb hovered right over the bright, colorful app icon, a microscopic physical motion that dictated the trajectory of his entire day.

Then, he remembered the specific instructions from Day 0. *An anchor is not a tether. You hit these anchors whenever the windows open. If you get interrupted… you pause, handle the chaos, and then return to the anchor. The discipline is in the return.*

Nate looked at the glowing green numbers on the microwave clock. He had exactly twelve minutes before he needed to log in for a highly demanding 7:00 AM sync with his engineering team.

He had a distinct, incredibly clear choice. He could let his terrible, sleep-deprived mood dictate his actions, declare Day 1 a total, embarrassing failure, scroll mindlessly for twelve minutes to soothe his bruised ego, and carry a dark, heavy cloud of resentment into his workday. Or, he could accept the stark, unvarnished reality of the morning, that it was messy, loud, and completely out of his control, and act on his intention anyway.

Nate put his phone down on the counter, face down. He didn't make a slow pour-over coffee; he poured a glass of cold tap water from the sink. He didn't go out to the picturesque back porch; he sat down right there on the hard linoleum kitchen floor, his back resting against the lower wooden cabinets, listening to the muffled, chaotic sounds of the cartoon playing in the next room. It wasn't Instagram-worthy. It wasn't beautiful. No one was going to applaud him for it. But it was intensely real.

He pulled up the day's precepts on his phone, ignoring the notification badges. *Acknowledge reality exactly as it presents itself, without demanding it be different before you act.*

Nate took a deep breath. The floor was hard and cold against his spine. He was deeply tired. It wasn't perfect. But for the very first time in months, he wasn't running away. He was fighting in the mud.

Track B: Cole's Morning

At exactly 0500, Cole's heavy boots hit the pavement at the end of his driveway.

The pre-dawn air was freezing, biting sharply at his exposed cheeks and the bare knuckles of his hands. He didn't flinch. This was his chosen environment; this was where he proved his superiority over the softer men still sleeping inside their warm, comfortable houses. His fifteen-minute silence walk was flawless. No music, no podcasts, just the rhythmic, crunching sound of gravel underfoot and the steady, measured expansion of his lungs in the dark.

By 0600, he was sitting at his meticulously organized, minimalist desk in the den, studying the precepts with a yellow highlighter in hand. *Accept reality.* Easy, he thought confidently. He built complex, multi-million dollar supply chains for a living; he dealt in raw facts, hard data, and logistical realities all day. *Drop the chase for comfort.* Also incredibly easy. He hadn't eaten a carb past 6:00 PM in five years, and he actively thrived on the brutal, tearing friction of heavy iron in the gym. *Act on intention, not mood.* Check. Cole prided himself above all else on never letting "how he felt" stop him from doing exactly what needed to be done. Emotions were a weakness he had largely trained out of himself.

At 0630, he moved to the freezing garage for his Practice Block. He knocked out a punishing, lung-burning kettlebell circuit, the cold air burning his throat with every inhalation. His heart rate was perfectly calibrated. By 0715, he was showered, dressed in a sharp, perfectly pressed button-down, and packing his leather briefcase. Track B was functioning exactly like a well-oiled machine.

Then, heavy, frantic footsteps pounded down the stairs.

His sixteen-year-old son, Jackson, appeared in the kitchen door-way. His hair was a chaotic mess, his backpack was slung slop-pily over one shoulder, and he looked panicked, holding a piece of burnt toast. "Dad, my alarm didn't go off. I missed the bus. I need a ride."

Cole froze, his hand tightening on the handle of his briefcase. His mental schedule mapped his precise departure for 0730, allowing him to bypass the absolute worst of the interstate traffic and arrive at the office exactly fifteen minutes early to prep for a critical director's meeting. Taking Jackson all the way to the high school would detour him directly into the gridlock. He would undoubtedly be late. He would look unprofessional.

A familiar, burning heat rose in Cole's chest. It was the quiet, intimidating anger he used to bend the world to his will and force compliance from his subordinates. He glared at his son, his voice dropping an octave, heavy with deep judgment. "Your alarm didn't go off, or you stayed up until 2:00 AM playing Xbox after I explicitly told you to go to sleep?"

Jackson looked down at the floor, his jaw tightening in defense, shrinking back from his father's intensity. The panic in his eyes shifted to familiar resentment. "Just... never mind. Forget it. I'll figure out how to walk in the cold."

"Get in the truck," Cole barked, grabbing his keys off the hook with a sharp, metallic clatter.

The twenty-minute drive to the high school was agonizingly, suffocatingly silent. The tension in the cab of the truck was thick enough to choke on. Cole gripped the steering wheel, his knuckles stark white, staring straight ahead at the bumper in front of him, refusing to look at his son. He was furious. Not just because he was going to be late to work, but because his perfect, disciplined, highly controlled morning had been casually compromised by someone else's laziness and total lack of structure.

At 1200, Cole sat alone in his office, staring blindly at a spreadsheet, initiating his Midday Reset. A strict ten-minute disconnection block.

He closed his laptop. He pushed his chair back. He closed his eyes. He forced himself to breathe deeply, inhaling for a count of four, holding, exhaling.

And as the thick adrenaline of the morning finally settled and cleared from his bloodstream, the stark reality of what had actually happened in the truck hit him like a physical blow to the stomach.

He thought back to the precepts he had read at 0600 with such smug, unearned confidence. *Act on intention, not mood.* What was his true, deepest intention with his son? If asked, Cole would say his intention was to raise a capable, resilient man and to maintain a strong, unbreakable relationship so his son would trust him when things got hard. But had he acted on that intention this morning? Absolutely not. He had acted entirely on his mood, a mood of rigid, inflexible irritation because his perfectly controlled schedule had been momentarily dented. He had chosen his spreadsheet over his son's trust.

He thought about the second precept. *Drop the chase for comfort.* Cole had always comfortably assumed "comfort" meant sitting on a plush couch eating junk food, watching television, or avoiding hard physical work. But sitting in the profound quiet of his office, he realized a horrifying truth: his rigid, punishing routine *was* his comfort. Being in total, unquestioned control was his specific dopamine hit. It made him feel safe in a world that had felt wildly unsafe since his divorce. When Jackson asked for a ride, Cole hadn't just lost fifteen minutes of time; he had lost his psychological safety blanket of control. His brooding, terrifying anger in the truck was just a middle-aged tantrum because he felt uncomfortable and out of control.

He hadn't accepted the reality of raising an imperfect, messy teenager. He was demanding a fantasy where a sixteen-year-old boy operated exactly like a seasoned, disciplined military subordinate.

Cole opened his eyes. The perfect morning was a total lie. He had failed Day 1 before 8:00 AM.

He pulled out a yellow sticky note and grabbed his favorite pen. He had a vital decision to make right now. He could bury the realization, double down on his facade of toughness, and keep playing the role of the stoic, unbreakable commander who was always right. Or, he could accept reality, drop his massive ego, and hit reset.

Cole wrote a quick text to Jackson. *I was wrong to take my frustration out on you in the truck this morning. I let a minor change in my schedule ruin my mood and dictate how I treated you. That's entirely on me, and I apologize. Have a good practice today. - Dad.*

He hit send. Pressing that button felt wildly, deeply uncomfortable. It felt like walking into enemy fire. It felt like the actual, grinding work of the retreat had finally begun.

The 3 Precepts of the Day

P1: Accept Reality

 **Practice Rendering:** Acknowledge reality exactly as it presents itself, without demanding it be different before you act.

The Trap: We mistakenly think acceptance means passive surrender, giving up, or pretending a bad situation is actually good or "happening for a reason." When something goes wrong, we spend massive amounts of cognitive energy screaming internally, "This shouldn't be happening," or "It's not fair," or "I didn't plan for this."

The Way Out: Acceptance simply means stopping the exhausting, invisible mental argument with the facts on the ground. By dropping the demand for reality to match your fantasy, you immediately conserve the cognitive energy you desperately need to actually solve the problem.

- **Modern Example:** A key supplier abruptly backs out of a contract, completely ruining a quarter you spent six months perfectly planning. Instead of pacing your office, venting to coworkers, and raging at the supplier's incompetence for two hours, you immediately accept the new board state, open your contingency file, and start dialing backups before your competitors do.

P2: Drop the Chase for Comfort

 **Practice Rendering:** Stop chasing temporary dopamine hits to escape the discomfort of the present moment.

The Trap: We assume this means we must live like ascetic monks and can never enjoy a cold beer, a good meal, or a movie ever again. In modern life, we rarely use comfort just for pleasure; we use it as an anesthetic. When we feel the friction of stress, boredom, or difficult tasks, we reflexively reach for our phones, sugar, or alcohol to numb the sensation.

Furthermore, for some highly structured people, maintaining rigid control is their own form of insulating comfort that prevents them from dealing with chaos.

The Way Out: Recognize the specific moments you are using pleasure or rigid control as an escape hatch from reality. When the friction hits, do not run. Sit in the fire.

- **Modern Example:** Catching yourself mindlessly opening Instagram or a news site for the fourth time in ten minutes while struggling to write a difficult, politically sensitive email. You notice the deep, bodily urge to escape the mental friction, and you intentionally put the phone in another room to break the loop and force yourself to sit with the discomfort of the blinking cursor.

P3: Act on Intention, Not Mood

 **Practice Rendering:** Base your actions on clear, decided intention, not fluctuating moods or half-hearted impulses.

The Trap: We falsely believe that we need to "feel motivated" before we can do hard work. We wait for inspiration to strike. Alternatively, we think discipline means completely burying our emotions and pretending we are feelingless robots. When we are tired, angry, or sad, we let those biological states dictate how we treat others and how we perform.

The Way Out: Fully recognize your emotions, know that you are exhausted, terrified, or furious, but utterly refuse to let those temporary biological states drive the car. Your mood is just a weather report; your intention is the map. You don't cancel a vital road trip just because it's raining; you just put on a heavier coat and drive more carefully.

- **Modern Example:** Feeling entirely drained, heavy, and foggy at 5:30 PM after a brutal day at the office, but actively choosing to sit on the floor and build Legos for ten minutes anyway, because your core intention is connection with your children, regardless of your current physical energy level.

Daily Practices

Choose *one* of these practices to execute during your Morning or Midday Anchor today.

Practice 1: The "What Is" Drill (3 Minutes) The next time something goes wrong today, a spilled coffee, a highly passive-aggressive email from a boss, a canceled meeting you prepared hours for, or unexpected traffic, you are not allowed to complain or express frustration for three full minutes. Instead, objectively state the physical reality of the situation out loud, like a detached, emotionless scientist recording data in a logbook.

- *Example:* "There is coffee on my desk. It is dripping onto the floor. I need to get paper towels. I will wipe it up."

- *Purpose:* This practice brutally and effectively short-circuits the emotional, ego-driven spiral of "Why does this always happen to me?" It forces your brain out of the emotional center and moves you immediately into the prefrontal cortex, the realm of rapid action and problem-solving.

Practice 2: The Urge Surf (5 Minutes) Sit in a chair with absolutely nothing in your hands. Do not look at a screen. Notice the physical sensation of wanting to check your phone, get a sugary snack, or find a distraction from the silence. Do not fight the urge, but do not act on it. Recognize it for exactly what it is: an escape hatch from boredom or stress. Just watch the desire to escape rise in your chest, peak in intensity, and then slowly fade away like a wave breaking on a beach.

- *Purpose:* To neurologically prove to your brain that an uncomfortable urge is just a passing biological sensation, not a hardwired command you must blindly obey. You are systematically building your tolerance to friction.

Practice 3: The Intention Check (Active) Before entering any new environment today (walking into the house after work, logging onto a Zoom call, entering the gym), pause for five seconds. State your primary intention for the next hour out loud.

- *Example:* "My intention is to listen without interrupting." or "My intention is to push to muscle failure."

- *Purpose:* This prevents your current mood from bleeding into the next room. It draws a hard line between your passive feelings and your active choices.

Evening Anchor: Journal Prompts

Tonight, clear away all distractions. Put your phone in another room. Set a timer for 10 minutes and answer these honestly. Do not write what you think sounds "disciplined." Write the ugly truth.

1. Where did I waste valuable cognitive energy today aggressively arguing with reality instead of just dealing with the facts on the ground?

2. When the day got stressful or boring, what was my default "escape hatch" (social media, junk food, snapping in anger, zoning out), and what specific emotional discomfort was I trying to run away from?

3. Did I let a temporary, passing mood dictate how I treated someone important to me today? How did it affect them?

4. If I had operated entirely on my core *intentions* today instead of my fleeting impulses, what specific moments or interactions would have looked radically different?

5. Where can I realistically expect reality to be messy or difficult tomorrow, and how will I prepare my mind to accept it without a tantrum?

Your Carry Card for Tomorrow

Write these lines on a small piece of paper or an index card. Carry it in your pocket or place it directly on your keyboard for Day 2.

Stop arguing with what is. Deal with what is. Notice the escape hatch. Mood is weather. Intention is the compass.

Close: You survived Day 1. You stepped into the mud and you didn't run from it. You proved you can act with intention even when the environment is hostile, the plan falls apart, and your mood is poor. But accepting reality is only the very first step of the retreat. Tomorrow, we are going to look incredibly closely at what is actively pulling you off the path.

Tomorrow, we confront the crushing weight of desire, the trap of dopamine, and the things you falsely think you "need" to be happy.

DAY 2:

DESIRE AND DOPAMINE

Desire is the primary, roaring engine of modern dissatisfaction. We are told relentlessly, by every glowing screen, billboard, and highly tuned algorithm in our lives, that the next promotion, the next luxury purchase, the next viral validation online will finally make us feel "enough." We are trained from early childhood to chase the grade, the trophy, and the status symbol, explicitly tying our deepest worth to what we acquire and how we are perceived.

We chase outcomes. This is called the "Arrival Fallacy", the illusion that once we reach a specific goal, we will reach lasting happiness. We tie our very identities to the success of a project, the number looking back at us on a bathroom scale, or the level of respect we command when we walk into a room. When we get the outcome we desire, we feel a brief, intoxicating hit of dopamine. We feel like gods. But when we don't get it, we feel crushed, highly defensive, and utterly desperate to fix the deficit.

We end up building our entire lives around trying to nervously manipulate the external world to satisfy the fragile, endless demands of the ego.

But a life tied entirely to outcomes is an incredibly fragile life. It is built on sand. You cannot control what the leadership team ultimately decides in a closed-door meeting. You cannot control the traffic on the interstate. You cannot control the weather, the economy, or what other people think of you, no matter how perfectly you behave.

Today, we are going to cut the strings that make us puppets to these outcomes. We are going to look at the massive, exhausting weight we carry around every single day, the weight of our ego, the desperation for specific results, and the toxic habit of carrying the guilt of past mistakes into the present moment. Today is about learning how to work fiercely and deeply without becoming an emotional slave to the result.

Track A: Nate's Morning

Nate woke up on Day 2 feeling slightly more resilient. The chaotic, vomit-stained start to Day 1 had proven to him that he didn't need a perfectly aesthetic environment to act with intention. He had survived the mud. But today was different. Today, the professional stakes were incredibly high.

He had a 10:00 AM meeting to pitch a massive new product feature he'd been designing and obsessing over for two straight months. It was his baby. He had poured his nights and weekends into the wireframes. He needed the VP of Product, Marcus, to look at it, completely validate his hard work in front of his peers, and tell the entire room it was a brilliant, game-changing direction for the company. Nate desired that outcome intensely. He physically craved the dopamine hit of being the smartest, most essential guy in the room. His ego was profoundly hungry.

That intense pressure immediately hijacked his morning routine. At 6:30 AM, while frantically trying to get out the door, he couldn't find his presentation clicker. His wife, Claire, was managing the toddler's messy breakfast and casually asked Nate a simple logistical question about their upcoming weekend plans with her parents.

"I don't know, Claire, I have a massive pitch today, can you just handle it?" Nate snapped, his voice sharp, tight, and dripping with dismissive arrogance. He grabbed his keys off the counter and walked out to the garage without making eye contact or saying goodbye.

As soon as he got into his cold car and backed out of the driveway, the guilt hit him. It felt like a heavy, cold lead weight in the pit of his stomach. He drove the first ten minutes of his commute entirely lost in his head, replaying the harsh interaction over and over, viciously beating himself up. *Why do I always do that? I'm trying to be disciplined, I'm doing this retreat, and I can't even get out the door without being a jerk to my wife. I'm a fraud. I'm failing at everything.*

He pulled into the office parking lot. He had fifteen minutes before he needed to go inside the building. It was time for his Morning Anchor.

Nate pulled out his phone and opened the precepts for Day 2. He read Precept 6: *Extract the operational lesson from past mistakes and immediately drop the emotional weight.* He paused, staring at the screen. Nate usually wore his guilt like a twisted badge of honor, subconsciously thinking that feeling terrible about snapping at Claire somehow made up for the bad behavior.

It was his penance. But Musashi was brutally clear: guilt is only a useful signal for about five minutes. It tells you that you violated your own standard. After that, it's just ego-driven, self-indulgent noise that keeps you focused on yourself and prevents you from taking new action. It was a massive emotional debt he was needlessly paying daily interest on.

Nate put the car in park. He extracted the raw, operational lesson: *I cannot let my desire for a specific work outcome bleed into how I speak to my family. That is a massive failure of boundaries, and I must separate the two domains.* Then, he took immediate action to burn the regret. He texted Claire: *I was completely out of line snapping at you about the weekend. I let the stress of this pitch make me a jerk. I am very sorry, and I'll make it right tonight.* He hit send. The emotional weight lifted almost instantly. The regret was burned, the debt was paid, and his focus returned to the present battlefield.

At 10:00 AM, Nate walked confidently into the boardroom. He was ready to dazzle. He began presenting the new feature, clicking smoothly through his carefully designed, highly polished slides. But as he spoke, he noticed a shift in his tone; he wasn't just explaining the work, he was defending it aggressively against invisible criticism. When Sarah, a highly capable junior designer, tried to politely point out a genuine flaw in the user flow on slide four, Nate immediately cut her off. He talked over her, deploying complex technical jargon to ensure the entire room knew he was the absolute authority. He was letting his ego drive the car to protect his desired outcome.

Marcus, the VP, leaned back in his chair, unimpressed. "Nate, it's just too heavy," he said bluntly, cutting right through the jargon. "The core idea is okay, but this interface is incredibly bloated. It's confusing. We aren't building this version. It needs to be cut in half before we even consider devoting engineering hours to it."

A sudden, physical rush of heat hit Nate's face. The public rejection stung deeply. His heart rate spiked. He desperately wanted to argue, to explain why Marcus was completely wrong, why Sarah couldn't grasp the broader vision, why his two months of grueling work couldn't just be dismissed with a wave of a hand. He felt completely, utterly enslaved by the outcome he had built up in his head. His identity was tied to those slides.

"Okay," Nate managed to say through tightly gritted teeth, staring at the table to hide his anger and the flush in his cheeks. "I'll... take another look."

The meeting ended awkwardly, the air entirely sucked out of the room. Nate walked back to his desk, his chest tight with deep frustration, defensiveness, and burning embarrassment.

At 12:30 PM, Nate slipped into an empty, glass-walled breakout room for his Midday Anchor. He pulled out the precepts.

He read Precept 4: *Shrink your ego and expand your awareness of the people and systems around you.* Then he read Precept 5: *Pursue your goals fiercely, without becoming emotionally enslaved by the outcome.*

Sitting in the quiet room, the stark reality of the morning washed over him. He had walked into that pitch demanding a specific result to stroke his ego and validate his worth as an employee. When he didn't get it, he instantly viewed his colleagues as enemies to be defeated. He hadn't been thinking lightly of himself; he had made himself the absolute main character of the entire company, falsely assuming his project was the center of the universe.

Nate had a decision to make. He could spend the rest of the day pouting at his desk, doing the bare minimum, and complaining bitterly to his work friends over Slack about how leadership "just didn't get it." Or, he could radically detach from the outcome, swallow his bruised pride, and focus purely on the effort of making the product better for the user.

Nate stood up. He walked directly over to Sarah's desk in the open floor plan, exposing himself to the very person he had snapped at.

"Hey," he said, keeping his voice calm, steady, and low. "I owe you a real apology. I talked over you in there because I was being highly defensive about my work. My ego was bruised. You were completely right about the user flow being clunky. Do you have ten minutes this afternoon to help me figure out how to cut this thing in half?"

Sarah looked surprised, her guard visibly dropping, then smiled. "Yeah, definitely. Let's pull it up on the whiteboard at two."

Nate didn't get the intoxicating dopamine hit of total victory, applause, and praise today. But as he sat down to revise the wireframes with Sarah, he realized he had secured something vastly better, deeper, and far more resilient: he had his equilibrium back.

Track B: Cole's Morning

At 0630, Cole was standing in his freezing garage, aggressively chalking his hands until his palms were white, the fine dust settling on his dark boots and the black rubber mats.

His Track B schedule called for his Practice Block, and today, that meant heavy, highly demanding deadlifts. Cole had been chasing a 405-pound personal record for three agonizing months. He had structured his strict diet, his rigid sleep schedule, and his entire lifting programming entirely around hitting this one specific number.

To Cole, pulling 405 pounds wasn't just a fun physical milestone or a fitness goal. It was undeniable proof. It was proof that at 46 years old, after a brutal divorce and years behind a desk, he was still a formidable, highly capable, dangerous man. It was proof that he wasn't losing his edge to age, decay, or a softer civilian life. He desired the outcome with a rigid, almost terrifying intensity. He needed the number to validate his identity and quiet the fear in his head.

He stepped up to the heavily loaded bar, the sharp steel knurling biting into his thick calluses. He locked his over-under grip, breathed in sharply, braced his core until it felt like a block of solid iron, and pulled with absolutely everything he had.

The bar broke the floor, climbed slowly, painfully halfway up his shins, and then hit an invisible, unmovable brick wall. His lower back began to round dangerously. His grip started to fail, his fingers uncurling against his will. No matter how hard he ground his teeth or strained his neck, the weight simply wasn't moving any higher.

He dropped the bar in total defeat. The 45-pound iron plates crashed against the rubber stall mats with a deafening boom that violently rattled the garage tools hanging on the pegboard wall.

Cole stood up, gasping for freezing air, and a massive wave of pure, red-hot fury hit him. He wanted to violently kick the heavy chalk bucket entirely across the garage. He wanted to scream at the wall. He felt physically weak, and to Cole, weakness of any kind was absolutely intolerable.

He took an aggressive step toward the bucket, his heavy boot raised to strike. Then, like a psychological circuit breaking, he remembered the reading block from 0600. Precept 5: *Pursue your goals fiercely, without becoming emotionally enslaved by the out-come.*

Cole froze mid-step. His chest was heaving. He realized with sudden, deeply uncomfortable clarity that he was acting exactly like a toddler throwing a tantrum because he didn't get the toy he wanted. He had put in the immense effort, he had trained hard, he had shown up consistently in the freezing cold, he hadn't skipped a single session. But he was utterly, helplessly enslaved by the result. His self-worth was literally tied to a metal bar and the unyielding gravitational pull of the earth.

Cole slowly, deliberately lowered his foot. "Control the effort. Surrender the result," he muttered out loud, his breath pluming in the cold air. He walked over to the bar, stripped the heavy plates off one by one, and quietly, methodically put them back on the rack. The deep disappointment was certainly still there, a dull ache in his chest, but the emotional spiraling, the destructive, ego-driven rage, stopped completely.

By 1000, Cole was sitting in his corner office dealing with a very different kind of heavy weight.

Six months ago, strictly against the explicit advice of his senior leadership team, Cole had hired a new project manager named Davis. It was Cole's call, overriding everyone else. And for the last three months, it had been glaringly, painfully obvious to everyone in the building that Davis was failing spectacularly. He was missing critical deadlines, angering clients, and actively costing the firm money.

Cole knew with absolute certainty he needed to fire him. But he had been dragging his feet for weeks. Why? Because firing Davis meant Cole had to publicly admit to his team that he made a bad hire. It meant admitting he was fallible, that his judgment was flawed, and that he was wrong. It was his massive ego, pure and simple, desperately protecting itself from the reality of a mistake, prioritizing his reputation over the health and survival of the company.

At 1200, Cole initiated his Midday Reset. He closed his laptop screen. He thought deeply about Precept 6: *Extract the operational lesson from past mistakes and immediately drop the emotional weight.* Cole realized he was choosing to pay a massive, daily tax on a mistake he made half a year ago. His fragile ego was making his own company bleed cash.

The ten-minute reset timer dinged. Cole opened his laptop, decisively drafted the termination paperwork without any hesitation, and called HR to schedule the meeting. At 1400, he brought Davis into his office and made the cut. He didn't blame Davis, he didn't get angry, he didn't make excuses or apologize profusely to soften the blow; he just stated the facts cleanly, offered a fair severance package, and executed the transition. The heavy, lingering dread he'd been carrying around his neck for weeks vanished instantly. He had burned the regret.

At 1600, his phone buzzed on his desk. It was a text from his sixteen-year-old daughter, Chloe.

Dad, I know tonight is my night to come over for steak and a movie, but Mia is having a major crisis and really needs me. Can I just go to her house instead? Can you drive me?

Cole stared hard at the glowing screen. The old Cole, the highly rigid Cole from just 48 hours ago, would have felt an immediate, burning flare of rejection. He would have rapidly replied: *It's my weekend. The schedule is set. Tell Mia you'll see her tomorrow.* He would have harshly enforced the boundary simply to protect his own desire to feel prioritized, respected, and wanted as a father.

But Cole remembered Precept 4. *Shrink the ego and expand your awareness.* He wasn't the main character of a sixteen-year-old girl's weekend. She wasn't maliciously rejecting him; she was being a loyal, good friend to someone who genuinely needed her. His rigid desire for his "perfectly scheduled dad time" was making him completely blind to her actual, evolving life and the highly emotional needs of her social circle.

Cole picked up the phone. He didn't type out a passive-aggressive guilt trip. He didn't coldly enforce the spreadsheet schedule.

I completely understand. I'll pick you up at 1800. We can grab a quick burger on the way to Mia's so we still get a few minutes together. Love you.

When he hit send, Cole fully expected to feel frustrated and angry that his quiet Friday night was ruined. Instead, as he packed up his briefcase to leave the office, he felt something entirely unfamiliar. He felt incredibly light.

The 3 Precepts of the Day

P4: Shrink the Ego, Expand the View

 **Practice Rendering:** Shrink your ego and expand your awareness of the people and systems around you.

The Trap: We mistakenly read Musashi's original "think lightly of yourself" as a mandate for self-deprecation, low self-esteem, or letting people walk all over you. We think it means being a doormat. But modern ego doesn't always look like arrogance; often, it looks like assuming every action taken by someone else is secretly about *you.*

The Way Out: It actually means taking yourself and your own desires far less seriously, so you can stop staring at your own reflection and pay better attention to the needs of the room. Ego acts like a blinder; shrinking it gives you vital peripheral vision to see what your team, your spouse, or your kids actually need.

- **Modern Example:** Recognizing that your deep obsession with maintaining your own rigorous, perfect weekend schedule is actively making your family's time with you highly stressful, and consciously choosing to bend your routine for them without holding onto resentment. You are not the main character of everyone else's day.

P5: Detach from the Outcome

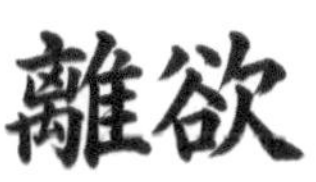 **Practice Rendering:** Pursue your goals fiercely, without becoming emotionally enslaved by the outcome.

The Trap: We fundamentally mistake detachment for apathy, laziness, or a lack of drive ("Who cares what happens? Nothing matters"). We think caring about the outcome is what motivates us to do the work. But when you tie your identity to a result you don't control, you become terrified of failure, which leads to corner-cutting, anxiety, and eventual burnout.

The Way Out: True detachment takes immense courage and vulnerability; it means caring deeply about the *effort*, pouring your absolute soul into the preparation, and acting with total ferocity, while completely accepting that the universe, the market, or the boss has absolute veto power over the final *result*.

- **Modern Example:** Pitching a new project you enthusiastically worked on for weeks. When leadership rejects it due to budget cuts, you take the feedback, extract the data, and calmly figure out the next step without taking the rejection as a devastating, crushing personal insult to your self-worth. Control the effort. Surrender the result.

P6: Drop the Weight of Regret

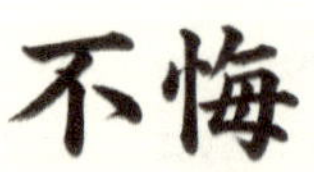 **Practice Rendering:** Extract the operational lesson from past mistakes and immediately drop the emotional weight.

The Trap: We think carrying guilt means we are good people. We think this precept means behaving like a sociopath who never admits fault or feels remorse. But wallowing in guilt is actually just a sneaky form of ego, it feels like penance, but it keeps you focused purely on your own feelings, preventing you from taking new, corrective action.

The Way Out: Refuse to pay daily emotional interest on a debt you've already settled. Guilt is an incredibly useful biological signal for exactly five minutes; it tells you your actions didn't match your values. Extract the data. Apologize. After that, it's just ego-driven self-indulgence that prevents new action.

- **Modern Example:** Snapping at your partner in the frantic morning rush because you are highly stressed about work. Instead of feeling deeply guilty all day and acting weird, distant, and defensive that night out of shame, you apologize directly and plainly at noon and reset the day. Extract the lesson. Burn the regret.

Daily Practices

Choose *one* of these practices to execute today.

Practice 1: The "Ego Check" Doorway Drill (Active) Every single time you walk through a physical doorway today to enter a new room (a meeting room, your kitchen, a gym, your boss's office), pause for one literal second. State internally: *"I am not the main character here. What does this room actually need from me?"*

- *Purpose:* This instantly and physically shifts your focus outward. It forcefully prevents you from dominating conversations to look smart, acting defensively, or taking innocent comments personally. It builds massive situational awareness.

Practice 2: Burn the Regret (5 Minutes) Take a physical piece of paper and a pen. Write down one highly specific mistake you made recently that is still causing you lingering guilt or frustration (a bad hire, a missed workout, a harsh word to a spouse, a financial error). Below it, write one single, objective sentence: "The operational lesson is [X]." Read the lesson out loud to yourself.

Then, physically tear the paper into tiny pieces and throw it in the trash. The debt is settled. Move on.

- *Purpose:* To externalize the internal monologue, process the failure logically rather than emotionally, and physically enact the process of letting it go.

Practice 3: The "Effort Only" Task (Execution) Identify one task today that you have been dreading because you are afraid of the outcome (making a difficult sales call, having a hard conversation, submitting a draft). Write down strictly what the *effort* looks like (e.g., "I will dial the number and read the script"). Execute the effort. Whatever the response is, you must silently say "Good" immediately after it concludes.

- *Purpose:* To sever the dopamine loop tied to getting a "yes" and re-tie it entirely to the act of doing the work.

Evening Anchor: Journal Prompts

Tonight, clear away all distractions. Put the phone in a drawer. Set a timer for 10 minutes and answer these honestly:

1. In what highly specific area of my life am I completely, hopelessly enslaved by the outcome (a promotion, a scale weight, a specific person's approval, a financial milestone)?

2. If I knew with 100% certainty I would fail at that goal, would the daily effort of pursuing it still be worth doing? Why or why not?

3. Did my fragile ego cause completely unnecessary friction, arguments, or drama for someone else today?

4. What past mistake am I continuing to pay daily emotional "interest" on, and what is the exact, unvarnished lesson I need to extract so I can drop it forever?

5. How specifically can I "shrink the ego" tomorrow morning before I interact with my family or coworkers?

Your Carry Card for Tomorrow

Write these lines on a small piece of paper or an index card. Carry it in your pocket or place it directly on your keyboard for Day 3.

You are not the main character. Control the effort. Surrender the result. Extract the lesson. Burn the regret.

Close: You have stopped arguing with reality, and you have started shrinking the massive, exhausting target of your own ego. You are no longer demanding that the world bend to your will. But intellectual insight without daily execution fades rapidly.

Tomorrow, we move deeper into the trenches. Day 3 is about confronting the things that actually break our discipline on a random Tuesday afternoon: the alluring poison of modern comparison, the toxic habit of complaining, and the brutal reality of holding the line. Get some sleep.

DAY 3:

COMPARISON, COMPLAINING, AND THE NOISE

If Day 1 was about accepting the mud of reality, and Day 2 was about unburdening your heavy ego, Day 3 is about actively plugging the massive leaks in your hull.

You only have a finite amount of cognitive and emotional energy to spend every single day. And yet, most of us unknowingly drill massive holes in our own gas tanks through two deeply toxic, incredibly common habits: constantly comparing our gritty, unedited reality to someone else's carefully curated highlight reel, and complaining out loud about circumstances we absolutely refuse to change.

Both of these destructive habits are rooted in a fundamental inability to accept impermanence and reality. We compare our lives to others because we cling tightly to the false idea that we should have "arrived" at success by now, viewing life as a frantic race with a finish line. We complain endlessly because we cling to a nostalgic, fictional fantasy of how easy life used to be, or a delusion of how easy it *should* be right now.

Today, we are going to learn how to keep our eyes locked firmly in our own boat. We are going to look at professional jealousy, social media envy, and casual complaining not just as bad manners or character flaws, but as massive, critical strategic errors that completely destroy your capacity for discipline. When you are looking at another man's life, you are not building your own.

Track A: Nate's Morning

Nate woke up feeling remarkably steady. His Morning Anchor was functioning just as designed. The house was relatively quiet, with only the low hum of the refrigerator. He poured his coffee, sat at the kitchen island, and completed his reading block with actual focus. It felt like he was finally finding his rhythm on this retreat.

Then, out of pure, unthinking muscle memory, he opened his laptop and clicked over to LinkedIn while taking a casual sip of coffee.

The very first post on his feed was from a guy named Greg. Greg was a product manager Nate had worked closely with three years ago. They had been at the exact same level, fighting for the same promotions, suffering through the same bad meetings. Now, Greg was posting a lengthy, agonizingly humble-brag announcement about how a boutique tech startup he co-founded had just been acquired for $15 million. The post included a high-resolution, professionally shot picture of Greg looking incredibly rested, deeply tanned, and standing casually on a sleek office balcony overlooking the ocean.

Nate felt the wind get completely knocked out of him.

The steady, grounded feeling from his Morning Anchor vanished instantly, entirely replaced by a dark, sinking wave of profound inadequacy. *Fifteen million dollars,* Nate thought, his heart rate ticking up. The artificial glow of the screen illuminated his tired face. He looked up from the laptop and looked around his kitchen.

There was a dried smear of peanut butter on the counter from yesterday. His mortgage was painfully high. His career, which he had felt somewhat proud of yesterday, suddenly felt like a slow-moving, embarrassing joke. He felt like he was losing a game he didn't even know he was playing.

A few minutes later, his wife Claire walked into the kitchen, looking thoroughly exhausted from a rough, sleepless night dealing with the toddler's teething. She was already mentally calculating the logistics of the day.

"Morning," she said flatly, opening the fridge to look for milk. "Did you remember to take the trash out to the curb like I asked last night?"

"No, I didn't," Nate snapped, his voice sharp with wildly misplaced anger. "I'm dealing with a lot right now, Claire. I just saw Greg sold a company for fifteen million dollars. Meanwhile, I'm going to spend my entire day begging middle management to approve a minor software patch just to justify my salary. This company is a joke. I'm falling so far behind everyone else."

Claire paused, the milk carton heavy in her hand, and looked at him. She didn't look sympathetic to his existential career crisis. She just looked incredibly tired of carrying the domestic load while he panicked about his status. "Okay, Nate. Well, the trash truck is coming in exactly ten minutes. So you're either going to take it out, or we're going to smell dirty diapers all week."

She walked out of the kitchen. Nate stood there alone, his chest tight with defensive resentment. He had just done exactly what Precept 9 warned strictly against: *Eliminate whining; it is a passive, toxic refusal to solve the problem in front of you.*

Nate looked down at his glowing phone. He actively remembered his Day 3 precepts. *Recognize that comparing your path to another's wastes the exact energy needed to build your own.*

He was leaking energy everywhere. Comparing his messy, unedited, chaotic Tuesday morning to Greg's singular, highly-curated, once-in-a-lifetime exit event was completely absurd. It was comparing apples to a mirage. It didn't put a single dollar in his bank account. It didn't make him a more present father. It just made him incredibly bitter and useless in the present moment.

Furthermore, complaining to his deeply exhausted wife about a job that successfully paid their mortgage didn't magically fix his career trajectory; it just added completely unnecessary weight to her already heavy mental load.

Nate closed the laptop with a definitive snap. He took a deep breath, tied up the overflowing trash bag, and hauled it out to the curb just as the loud diesel engine of the truck rounded the corner. When he walked back inside, he didn't go back to his laptop to keep scrolling. He went straight upstairs to find Claire.

"I'm sorry I complained and snapped at you," he said, keeping his voice steady and owning the mistake. "You're tired, I'm tired. Greg's money has absolutely nothing to do with us or our life. I've got my eyes in my own boat."

Track B: Cole's Morning

By mid-morning on Day 3, Cole's highly rigid Track B schedule was executing flawlessly, like running code. He had hit his 0500 silence walk in the bitter cold, completely crushed his garage workout, and was currently aggressively chewing through a massive stack of operational reports at his mahogany desk.

His phone vibrated against the wood. It was a text from his sixteen-year-old daughter, Chloe.

Hey Dad, about our Saturday hike this weekend… do you mind if we skip it? A bunch of the girls from the volleyball team are going to the mall and I really want to go with them. Sorry!

Cole stared hard at the screen. Since his messy, painful divorce three years ago, the early Saturday morning hike with Chloe had been an immovable, sacred pillar in his life. It was *their* thing. It was the only time all week she actually put her phone in her pocket and talked to him about her life without distractions.

A sharp, incredibly familiar sting hit the back of his throat. He read Precept 8 that morning during his reading block: *Accept that loss and transition are natural, and let go with grace instead of clinging to what was.* But Cole didn't want to let go. He wanted to cling with both hands. His mind immediately and predictably went to a dark place of deep, toxic comparison. He thought bitterly about his ex-wife's new husband, a guy named Rick who drove a flashy speedboat and took the kids water-skiing on his alternating weekends.

Rick didn't do "character-building morning hikes." Rick didn't demand eye contact or deep conversations. Rick did fun. Rick was easy.

Of course she wants to skip the hike with me, Cole thought bitterly, staring blankly at his complex spreadsheet without seeing the numbers. *I'm the strict, boring dad who makes her sweat and wake up early, and everyone else gets to be the fun dad. It's completely unfair. I do all the hard, grinding parenting work to build her character, and Rick gets all the easy rewards.*

Cole sat paralyzed at his desk for twenty minutes, silently complaining to himself, letting a dark, toxic resentment boil in his chest. He was actively drafting a text message in his head to send back to Chloe, a highly passive-aggressive, guilt-inducing note about how "commitment to family is important," how she was breaking a tradition, and how deeply disappointed he was that she was choosing the mall over him.

At 1200, his daily alarm went off for his Midday Reset.

Cole slowly closed his laptop and stepped entirely away from the desk. He stood in the center of the office and closed his eyes. The profound silence of the room hit him, and the stark reality of his own petty thoughts echoed back loudly.

He was actively comparing himself to Rick. He was whining internally about the fundamental "fairness" of parenting.

Everything has a season, Musashi's rule stated clearly. *Let it go gracefully.*

Cole realized the hard, unavoidable truth: the specific era of the mandatory Saturday morning father-daughter hike was naturally ending. Chloe was sixteen. It was completely natural, highly normal, and entirely inevitable that she wanted to spend her weekends socializing with her peers. It had absolutely nothing to do with Rick buying her affection, and nothing to do with Cole being a "bad" or boring dad.

It was just the painful reality of impermanence. She was growing up. Actively fighting it, trying to guilt-trip her into compliance, and complaining bitterly about it wouldn't magically make her want to hike with him; it would just make her deeply resent his rigidity and push her further away.

Cole opened his eyes. He picked up his phone, deleted the passive-aggressive draft he had started to type, and took a breath.

No problem at all, kiddo, he typed quickly. *Have a great time at the mall with the team. I'll pick you up some of that spicy tuna sushi you like for dinner on Sunday instead.*

He hit send and put the phone face down. The sharp sting of loss was certainly still there in his chest, he was going to miss those quiet hikes on the trail terribly, but the toxic, heavy bitterness was completely gone. He had let the season transition with grace, protecting the relationship over his own ego.

The 3 Precepts of the Day

P7: Kill Comparison

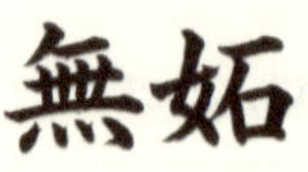 **Practice Rendering:** Recognize that comparing your path to another's wastes the exact energy needed to build your own.

The Trap: We assume jealousy is just about coveting vast amounts of money, sports cars, or extreme status. More often, modern comparison is being secretly, deeply jealous of someone else's apparent ease, their abundant free time, or their seeming lack of daily friction. We relentlessly compare our gritty, unedited, exhausting, behind-the-scenes reality to someone else's highly curated, heavily filtered highlight reel.

The Way Out: Recognize that every minute you spend looking at someone else's success is a minute you aren't building your own. You must radically accept that you are running a different race, with different starting conditions. Keep your eyes locked entirely in your own boat.

- **Modern Example:** Scrolling LinkedIn or Instagram on the couch and seeing a college friend sell a startup or buy a house. Feeling an immediate, sinking pang of deep inadequacy, but actively catching the thought, closing the app immediately, and grounding yourself by focusing solely on the messy, real life right in front of you.

P8: Accept Impermanence

別離 **Practice Rendering:** Accept that loss and transition are natural, and let go with grace instead of clinging to what was.

The Trap: We wrongly assume this requires a cold, robotic, or totally uncaring response to loss, grief, or major life changes. We think we have to pretend we aren't sad. But clinging to a past season, whether it's an old job title, a past relationship, or the toddler years of your children, causes immense suffering because you are demanding the universe run backwards.

The Way Out: It actually means allowing yourself to fully, deeply feel the sadness or nostalgia of a passing era without fighting the undeniable, structural reality that all things, good and bad, eventually end. Suffering comes from the clinging, not the changing.

- **Modern Example:** Realizing your growing child has reached an age where they no longer want to do a traditional weekend activity with you. You allow yourself to feel the sharp sting of the era passing, fully accept that they are growing up as they should, and offer a new way to connect instead of clinging desperately to the past.

P9: Eliminate Complaints

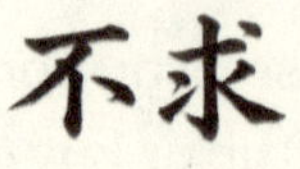 **Practice Rendering:** Eliminate whining; it is a passive, toxic refusal to solve the problem in front of you.

The Trap: We think this strict rule means we can't ever speak up about actual injustices, point out systemic flaws, or ask for necessary help. We confuse complaining with critique. You can and absolutely should critique, correct, and strategize. But *complaining* is entirely different, it is repeatedly voicing displeasure to an audience without any intent to take action. It is a highly addictive feedback loop of victimhood that drains your agency.

The Way Out: If you have the power to fix a situation, fix it. If you do not have the power to fix it, complaining about it is just adding negative noise to the world. Shut your mouth and get to work.

- **Modern Example:** Catching yourself standing in the breakroom venting for twenty consecutive minutes about upper management's universally poor communication. Realizing it changes absolutely nothing and drains your personal agency, so you abruptly cut the complaint short and pivot the team to a viable solution.

Daily Practices

Choose *one* of these practices to execute during your day.

Practice 1: The Complaint Fast (Active) For the next 12 straight hours, you are not allowed to voice a single complaint out loud about the weather, the traffic, your workload, the economy, or other people. If you catch yourself mid-complaint, you must immediately stop talking, mid-sentence, and say out loud, "But I am choosing to handle it."

- *Purpose:* To ruthlessly expose exactly how much conversational energy you waste every day being a passive victim of your circumstances, and to force you to find other things to talk about.

Practice 2: The "Own Boat" Visualization (Mental Drill) The next time you feel a sudden pang of jealousy today, whether triggered by social media, hearing about a peer's recent success, or seeing a neighbor's new car, close your eyes for five literal seconds. Visualize yourself sitting in a small, sturdy rowboat on the water. Visualize looking over at a massive, gleaming yacht passing by. Then, physically turn your head forward, look down at your own oars, and imagine firmly gripping them.

- *Purpose:* To physically and mentally break the addictive cognitive loop of comparison and instantly return your focus to the only vehicle you actually control.

Practice 3: The Impermanence Audit (Mental Drill) Look around your living room or office. Pick one thing you deeply love (a pet, a child, a spouse, a quiet morning). Remind yourself, explicitly, that this exact dynamic will end. The pet will age, the child will move out, the morning will become busy.

- *Purpose:* Not to induce sadness, but to force a profound sense of gratitude for the exact season you are currently living in.

Evening Anchor: Journal Prompts

Tonight, clear away all distractions. Set a timer for 10 minutes and answer these honestly:

1. Who specifically did I compare myself to today, and what deep, underlying insecurity did that brief comparison trigger in me?

2. What is one specific "season" or phase of my life that is currently ending, and how am I stubbornly fighting that transition instead of accepting it gracefully?

3. What was the absolute most useless, energy-draining complaint that came out of my mouth today? Who did I say it to?

4. If I took all the mental energy I wasted complaining and comparing today and strictly applied it to a personal goal, what could I have accomplished?

5. Where specifically do I need to strictly keep my eyes in my own boat tomorrow?

Your Carry Card for Tomorrow

Write these lines on a small piece of paper or an index card. Carry it in your pocket or place it directly on your keyboard for Day 4.

Comparison is a thief. Keep your eyes in your own boat. Everything has a season. Let it go gracefully. If you can fix it, fix it. If you can't, complaining is noise.

Close: You have stopped the major leaks in the hull. You are slowly learning to protect your vital energy by dropping the fantasy, shrinking the ego, and refusing to complain. But as you build this internal, stoic fortress, the people around you will inevitably notice the change, and the external world will test you.

Tomorrow, we confront the hardest test of all: navigating relationships, setting firm boundaries without being cold, and surviving the brutal reality of flawed environments. Get some sleep.

DAY 4:

STATUS, ENVIRONMENT, AND THE CORE

For the first three days of this retreat, we have been fighting battles entirely inside your own head. We have dealt with your ego, your complaints, and your personal relationship with reality.

Today, the battlefield expands. Today, we deal with the external world.

One of the greatest threats to modern discipline is our deep, unyielding obsession with our physical environment and our social status. We genuinely believe the lie that our focus and our happiness are entirely dependent on our surroundings. We think, *If I just had a nicer, quieter office, a bigger house, or a better boss, I would finally be calm, productive, and disciplined.*

When the environment is inevitably flawed, when it is loud, chaotic, or uninspiring, we use it as a highly convenient excuse to break our discipline. It is a form of geographical cure, hoping the outside fixes the inside.

Similarly, we constantly allow the intoxicating rush of new things, a new romance, a brilliant new business idea, or the desire to impress a room full of powerful strangers, to completely override our foundational responsibilities. We abandon the people who need us most to chase a temporary high and the illusion of status. We let the fire burn down the house.

Today is about learning how to become environmentally bulletproof. It is about learning to anchor internally, cultivating absolute adaptability with whatever flawed tools you are handed, and violently protecting your core values when the dopamine of something "new" tries to pull you off the path.

Track A: Nate's Morning

It was Thursday. Nate was working from home, and the house was an absolute disaster zone.

His five-year-old was home sick from kindergarten, watching television at maximum volume in the living room. His wife, Claire, was on a high-stakes, "do not disturb" zoom call in the bedroom with the door shut. Nate was relegated to the small, wobbly kitchen table, trying to finish a critical data report that was due to his director at noon.

To survive the noise of his house, Nate relied heavily on his expensive, over-ear noise-canceling headphones. They were his lifeline. They created the artificial, perfectly silent "cave" he needed to focus on complex tasks. But at 9:15 AM, right in the middle of a complex spreadsheet formula, the headphones beeped twice and abruptly died. He had forgotten to charge them the night before.

The wall of noise hit him instantly. The cartoon blared from the living room. The dog was barking frantically at the mailman through the front window. The refrigerator was humming loudly.

Nate felt a massive, immediate surge of frustration. *I literally cannot work in these conditions,* he thought, slamming his hands down on the table, making his coffee spill slightly. *It is impossible to be a professional in this house. I need an actual office. This environment is completely toxic to my productivity. How am I supposed to succeed here?*

He stood up, ready to storm down the hall, interrupt Claire's call, and aggressively complain about the noise level. He wanted to blame his lack of focus entirely on his surroundings. He wanted to be a victim of the noise.

Then, he remembered his Morning Anchor reading. Precept 11: *Cultivate the adaptability to work with whatever tools, conditions, or circumstances you are handed.* And Precept 12: *Find peace and focus internally, regardless of your external environment or its flaws.*

Nate stopped dead in the hallway. He realized he was acting incredibly fragile. He was acting like a man who required a perfect, curated, multi-million dollar laboratory just to do his basic job. If his entire concept of discipline and focus shattered the second a lithium-ion battery died, it wasn't discipline at all; it was just a luxury preference.

Nate turned around and walked to the junk drawer in the kitchen. He dug through old batteries, takeout menus, and rubber bands until he found a pair of cheap, neon-orange foam earplugs left over from a concert years ago. He rolled them up, shoved them deep in his ears, and sat back down at the kitchen table. The environment was still chaotic. It wasn't perfectly silent. It wasn't perfect. But he anchored his focus internally, stared hard at the spreadsheet, and forced himself to adapt. He finished the report with twenty minutes to spare.

Later that evening, after the kids were finally asleep, Nate experienced a totally different kind of threat.

He was sitting on the couch, brainstorming, when he was suddenly hit with an absolutely brilliant idea for a side-hustle app. The concept was so clear, so obviously profitable, that his brain flooded with a massive wave of dopamine. He felt an intoxicating rush of energy. He wanted to sprint into his office, lock the door, pull an all-nighter, and start coding the prototype immediately to chase the high.

But he had made a firm promise to Claire on Day 2. He had promised her that tonight, Thursday night, would be a phone-free, laptop-free evening for just the two of them to reconnect after a brutal week.

The internal tug-of-war was agonizing. The new idea felt urgent, exciting, and full of potential status and wealth. Sitting on the couch watching a movie with his wife felt mundane, slow, and boring by comparison.

He thought of Precept 10: *Love deeply, but do not let infatuation or emotional highs compromise your core values or judgment.*

Nate's core value was his marriage. The app idea was an infatuation, a shiny new toy, a burning fire. If he abandoned Claire right now to chase the high of a new project, he would be proving, through his actions, that his ambition and his desire for status were more important than his word and his family.

Nate grabbed a single index card, wrote down the core concept of the app in three quick sentences so he wouldn't forget it, and left the card on his desk. He walked back into the living room, sat down next to Claire, and picked up the TV remote. The app could wait until tomorrow. The fortress held.

Track B: Cole's Morning

Cole was on the road. His Track B schedule dictated rigid precision, but his travel schedule dictated complete chaos.

He woke up at 0500 in a sterile, generic corporate hotel room in Chicago. It was time for his Practice Block. He put on his gym clothes, rode the elevator down to the basement level, and opened the glass door to the hotel fitness center.

It was a total disaster. The room was the size of a large closet. The air smelled like old carpet. The single treadmill had an "Out of Order" sign taped over the screen. The dumbbell rack was entirely missing the 30, 40, and 50-pound weights, leaving only light pink dumbbells and a single 70-pounder.

Cole stood in the doorway, feeling a wave of rigid, arrogant disgust. *This is a joke,* he thought. *I can't train in this. It completely throws off my entire programming block. It's sub-optimal. I'll just skip it and double up on Saturday when I'm back in my own garage where things are correct.*

He turned to leave, fully prepared to take the easy out. But the reading from 0600 flashed in his mind like a warning light. Precept 11: *Cultivate adaptability.* Cole realized his "hardcore" garage gym routine had actually made him incredibly soft and highly dependent. He was utterly reliant on heavy barbells, perfect bumper plates, and a specific temperature to feel like he was doing the work. Faced with suboptimal conditions, his first instinct was to complain and completely quit.

"The perfect setup is a myth," Cole muttered to himself, stepping into the room.

He dropped his towel, walked into the empty space in the middle of the room, and set the timer on his watch for exactly 30 minutes. He executed a brutal, unbroken circuit of maximum-effort burpees, jump squats, and decline pushups with his feet elevated on a broken bench. He used the single 70-pound dumbbell for goblet squats until his legs shook. By minute 25, he was in a pool of sweat, his heart hammering against his ribs. He had adapted. He had used exactly what was in front of him. He was environmentally bulletproof.

That evening, Cole faced a much more complex, subtle test of his core.

He had a highly important dinner meeting with three VIP clients. The dinner went exceptionally well. At 9:00 PM, the clients ordered another round of expensive drinks, lit cigars, and invited Cole to join them at an exclusive, high-end bar downtown to keep the night going.

Cole felt the heavy, magnetic pull of status. These were powerful, wealthy men. Going with them would secure his reputation as a "player" in the industry. It would stroke his ego. It was the exact kind of professional infatuation that used to dictate his entire life before his divorce, when he constantly prioritized networking over being home.

But Cole had a firm boundary written into his Track B schedule. His Evening Reflection and his daily nightly phone call to his teenagers happened at 2000 hours. He was already an hour late.

Guard your core values, Precept 10 demanded.

The old Cole would have enthusiastically ordered another drink, texted his kids a quick, dismissive "busy at work, talk tomorrow," and spent the next three hours chasing the approval and status of men who didn't actually care about him if the contract fell through.

Cole stood up from the table. He smiled warmly and shook their hands, looking them in the eye. "Gentlemen, the dinner was fantastic, and the deal is solid. But I have an ironclad commitment to call my kids before they go to sleep, and I have an early morning. The next round is on me. Have a great night."

The clients looked mildly surprised, they were used to people bending over backward for them, but they nodded with genuine respect. A man who holds his boundaries is far more respected than a man who begs for approval.

Cole walked out of the restaurant and into the cold Chicago air. He walked back to his small, sterile hotel room. It wasn't the massive, comfortable family home he used to own. It was just a bed and a desk. But as he sat down, dialed his daughter's number, and opened his journal to complete his Evening Anchor, he didn't feel lonely or displaced. He had anchored internally. He was exactly where he chose to be.

The 3 Precepts of the Day

P10: Guard Your Core Values

 **Practice Rendering:** Love deeply, but do not let infatuation or emotional highs compromise your core values or judgment.

The Trap: We interpret this as a mandate to be a loveless, distant monk who never experiences joy or passion. But the real trap is letting the blinding, intoxicating rush of something "new", a new romance, lust, a status-driven networking event, or even extreme passion for a brand-new hobby, derail the foundational responsibilities, promises, and relationships you've already built.

The Way Out: Enjoy the fire of inspiration and passion, but build a firewall around your core duties. Do not let the new shiny object burn down the house you've spent years building.

- **Modern Example:** Feeling a massive, dopamine-fueled rush of excitement about a brand-new side hustle idea, but actively refusing to abandon your previously promised, phone-free evening with your spouse to chase the high. You write the idea down, and you return to your core.

P11: Cultivate Adaptability

Practice Rendering: Cultivate the adaptability to work with whatever tools, conditions, or circumstances you are handed.

The Trap: We mistake adaptability for having no standards or accepting mediocrity. We think we need the best gear to do the best work. You are allowed to have high-end preferences, but you cannot be *dependent* on them. If your morning routine, your workout, or your deep work shatters the second you lose your perfect conditions, your discipline is a fragile illusion.

The Way Out: Train yourself to execute in suboptimal conditions. Prove to your brain that the tool does not make the craftsman.

- **Modern Example:** Showing up to your hotel gym on a stressful business trip only to find broken equipment and zero space. Instead of skipping the workout because it's "suboptimal," you drop to the floor and execute a brutal, 30-minute bodyweight circuit. The perfect setup is a myth.

P12: Anchor Internally, Not Externally

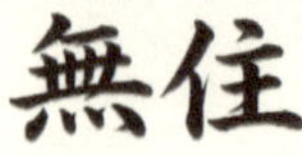 **Practice Rendering:** Find peace and focus internally, regardless of your external environment or its flaws.

The Trap: We assume this means you should be perfectly happy living in a dumpster or a toxic workplace. It actually targets the "geographical cure", the false, highly prevalent belief that moving to a bigger house, a cooler city, or getting a nicer office will magically fix your internal chaos.

The Way Out: Realize that if your mind is a storm, you will just bring the storm to the nicer house. Build your focus so deeply inward that external noise becomes entirely irrelevant.

- **Modern Example:** Being forced to move from a large, comfortable home into a much smaller apartment after a financial hit or divorce. You consciously make the small space a place of deliberate calm and order, rather than letting it become a depressing monument to what you lost.

Daily Practices

Choose *one* of these practices to execute during your day.

Practice 1: The Suboptimal Drill (Active) Pick one task today that you normally require "perfect conditions" to complete (e.g., answering emails, reading, working out, sleeping). Intentionally sabotage the environment. If you usually need total silence, turn on the TV in the background or go to a loud coffee shop. If you usually need your favorite expensive pen, use a cheap hotel pencil. Complete the task anyway.

- *Purpose:* To forcefully break your psychological dependence on your environment and systematically prove that your focus comes from within, not from your gear or your surroundings.

Practice 2: The Status Veto (Decision Point) At some point today, you will be presented with a choice that strokes your ego or elevates your status, but subtly compromises a core value or a boundary (e.g., gossiping to fit in with coworkers, staying late at work just to be "seen" by the boss instead of going home to your family, buying something flashy on credit). You must identify this specific moment and actively veto it.

- *Purpose:* To practice choosing your character over your reputation in real-time, severing your dependence on external validation.

Practice 3: The "Wait 24 Hours" Rule (Mental Drill) When you feel a massive spike of infatuation today, an urge to buy a new piece of gear, start a massive new project, or entirely change your routine, write the idea down and completely ban yourself from acting on it for 24 hours.

- *Purpose:* To separate genuine inspiration from dopamine-driven infatuation.

Evening Anchor: Journal Prompts

Tonight, clear away all distractions. Set a timer for 10 minutes and answer these honestly:

1. What specific tool, environment, or "perfect condition" am I currently using as a comfortable excuse for my lack of progress?

2. How did I react the last time my environment was chaotic or suboptimal? Did I adapt and execute, or did I whine and shut down?

3. Where in my life am I currently infatuated (with a new idea, purchase, or a new person), and is that infatuation causing me to actively neglect my foundational duties?

4. Did I make any decisions today purely to look important or maintain status in front of other people?

5. How can I practice anchoring internally tomorrow when the external noise inevitably starts?

Your Carry Card for Tomorrow

Write these lines on a small piece of paper or an index card. Carry it in your pocket or place it directly on your keyboard for Day 5.

Enjoy the fire, but don't let it burn down the house. The perfect setup is a myth. Use what is in front of you. Your environment does not dictate your focus. You do.

Close: You have survived the external pressure. You are learning that your environment is just a backdrop, not your master. You are protecting your core from the intoxicating highs of status and infatuation. You are becoming a harder target to hit.

Tomorrow, we confront one of the most difficult and nuanced battlegrounds of all: how we consume, how we hoard, how we edit our lives, and how we interact with the heavy, unwritten default expectations of society. Get some sleep.

DAY 5:

CONSUMPTION, CLUTTER, AND THE DEFAULT

We are a heavily burdened, bloated society. We are saturated. Not just physically, though we often are, using heavily processed food and alcohol to numb our daily stress, but mentally and socially.

We constantly accumulate. We hoard physical possessions we don't use, convincing ourselves we might "need them someday." We maintain draining, toxic relationships simply out of habit and a fear of being alone. We blindly obey the "default" expectations of our industries, our families, and our peer groups without ever pausing to ask if those rules actually serve our mission. We cling to these things because they feel deeply familiar, and familiarity feels safe, even when it is actively destroying our potential.

But agility requires lightness. A warrior cannot fight while carrying a backpack full of rocks. If you want to be disciplined, you cannot carry a massive load of emotional, physical, and social garbage.

Today is about ruthless editing. We are going to strictly examine how you consume (both food and media), how much unnecessary clutter you are carrying, and the courage it takes to actively question the "default" way everyone else is living. We are going to look at relationships and obligations not as things to aggressively cling to, but as elements of our lives that must be intentionally curated.

Track A: Nate's Morning

It was Friday afternoon. The energy in Nate's office was practically vibrating with the frantic, restless desire for the weekend to begin.

At 3:00 PM, Nate hit the wall. He was staring at an email draft that felt completely impossible to write. His brain was sluggish, his eyes hurt from the screen, and he felt a low-level anxiety about a deadline. Right on schedule, a well-meaning coworker dropped a bright pink box of gourmet donuts on the center table of the open-plan office.

Nate's immediate, biological reaction was to stand up. *I need one of those,* he thought, his mouth actually watering. *I've had a brutal week. I deserve a treat. It will give me the energy to push through to five o'clock. It will make me feel better.*

He walked halfway to the table before he stopped. He remembered Precept 13: *Treat food primarily as fuel, breaking the habit of using comfort consumption to regulate your emotions.*

Nate paused and looked at the box. He wasn't physically hungry. His body didn't need fuel; he had eaten a large lunch. What he actually needed was a distraction from the uncomfortable friction of the difficult email waiting on his screen. He was trying to use sugar as a chemical escape hatch to manually regulate his stress. He turned around, walked to the breakroom, grabbed a glass of cold water, and went back to his desk. The email was still hard to write, but he didn't add a massive sugar crash and a wave of guilt to his problems. He faced the friction sober.

Two hours later, at 5:00 PM, the real test of his social courage began.

Every Friday, a group of managers from Nate's department went to a local sports bar for happy hour. It was the unquestioned "default" of his office culture. If you wanted to be seen as a team player, you went. But these happy hours were rarely joyful; they were almost entirely dedicated to twenty-minute complaint sessions about upper management, venting about impossible clients, and exchanging toxic, career-damaging gossip.

"You coming, Nate?" his coworker, Mark, asked, tossing his jacket over his shoulder. "First round is on me."

Nate felt the deep, instinctual, evolutionary pull to comply. He wanted to belong to the tribe. He didn't want to be the outcast. But he also knew the actual math of the situation: every time he went, he drank two beers he didn't really want, spent two hours absorbing deeply negative energy, and got home at 7:30 PM feeling irritable and exhausted, leaving Claire to handle the absolute worst part of the kids' bedtime routine entirely alone.

He thought of Precept 14: *Ruthlessly edit your physical and mental space.* And Precept 15: *Question the default... do what actually works, not what is merely expected.*

Why was he clinging to this specific social obligation? He was clinging to it out of fear, fear of missing out, fear of being judged by Mark and the others. It was an energy leak.

"Not tonight, Mark," Nate said cleanly, packing his laptop into his bag. "I've got to get home to Claire and the kids. Have a good weekend."

Mark looked slightly offended, shrugging his shoulders. "Suit yourself, man."

As Nate walked out to his car, he felt a brief pang of social anxiety, the fear of social rejection, but it was quickly entirely overshadowed by a profound sense of relief. He had successfully edited his life. He had discarded a broken default. He pulled into his driveway at 5:45 PM, exactly when his family needed him most, with a clear head and a full tank of energy to give them.

Track B: Cole's Morning

At 1830 on Friday, Cole was executing his evening routine with his usual, relentless precision.

He was standing in his pristine kitchen, eating his perfectly measured Track B dinner out of a glass container: exactly six ounces of unseasoned chicken breast, a cup of plain white rice, and steamed broccoli. He ate standing up, staring out the window into the dark yard, viewing the meal purely as a biological transaction to repair muscle tissue after his workout. Food was not joy; food was math.

In the adjacent living room, his sixteen-year-old son, Jackson, was sitting alone on the couch, silently eating a slice of delivery pizza and staring blankly at his phone.

The physical distance between them was only fifteen feet, but the emotional distance felt like a canyon. Cole chewed his dry chicken, watching his son. He felt a deep, gnawing sense of isolation that his rigid routine couldn't fully numb.

Cole thought deeply about Precept 13. *Fuel over comfort.* Cole had mastered this rule physically; he never used food for comfort. But as he looked at Jackson, Cole realized he had weaponized the rule. His hyper-strict, completely inflexible diet had become a fortress that actively prevented human connection. He was so terrified of losing his hard-earned physical edge, so attached to his identity as the "disciplined guy," that he couldn't just sit down, share a messy pizza with his kid on a Friday night, and talk about the week.

Question the default, Precept 15 challenged him. *Trust active observation over passive tradition.*

Cole's default was total, unyielding rigidity. But his observation told him that this rigidity was currently isolating him from his own blood.

Cole put his glass container of chicken back in the fridge. He walked into the living room, grabbed a paper plate, took a slice of pepperoni pizza from the greasy cardboard box, and sat down directly next to Jackson on the couch.

Jackson looked up from his phone, his eyes wide with genuine shock. "Dad? Are you... are you eating a carb?"

Cole smiled, a real, unforced smile that reached his eyes. "I figured I'd survive one slice. How was practice today?"

The ice broke. They spent the next hour actually talking, laughing, and connecting over a terribly greasy meal. Cole realized that discipline meant knowing exactly when to hold the line, but true wisdom meant knowing when to intentionally cross it for a higher purpose.

Later that night, Cole walked out to his freezing garage to finalize his Evening Anchor.

He looked over at the far corner of the garage. Stacked against the wall were five heavy, grey plastic bins. They contained his old military dress uniforms, faded deployment gear, commendations, and photo albums from the earliest, happiest years of his marriage. They had sat in that exact corner, unopened and gathering dust, for nearly four years.

Ruthlessly edit your physical and mental space, keeping only what serves your current mission, Precept 14 demanded.

Cole had been clinging to those boxes like a life raft. He was hoarding the physical evidence of his past identity because he was secretly terrified that his best, most honorable, most capable days were permanently behind him. The boxes were a massive physical manifestation of his refusal to accept impermanence. They were a sunk cost of identity.

Cole didn't hesitate. He didn't open the boxes to take a nostalgic trip down memory lane, knowing it would just trigger regret and longing. He walked over, picked up the heavy bins two at a time, and carried them out to the trunk of his truck. He would drop them off at a veteran's donation center first thing tomorrow morning.

He swept the empty corner of the garage floor clean. He stood in the newly created open space, breathing in the cold air. The garage felt larger. His mind felt infinitely lighter. He was finally ready for what was next.

The 3 Precepts of the Day

P13: Fuel Over Comfort

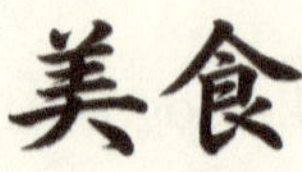 **Practice Rendering:** Treat food primarily as fuel, breaking the habit of using comfort consumption to regulate your emotions.

The Trap: We think we have to eat unseasoned chicken breast forever, adopting a punishing, miserable diet culture to be "disciplined." The trap isn't the food itself; the trap is using the food (or alcohol, or spending) as a chemical numbing agent to manually regulate our stress, anxiety, or boredom.

The Way Out: Break the deep emotional dependency on "treating yourself" just because you had a hard day. Eat to fuel your intended actions for tomorrow, not to numb the stress of today.

- **Modern Example:** Walking right past the box of 3 PM office donuts. Not because you are aggressively counting macros, but because you recognize you only want the donut because you are highly stressed about a deadline, and sugar won't write the report.

P14: Edit Your Life

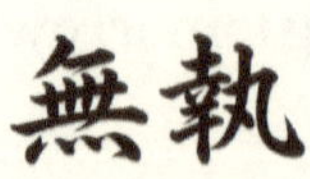 **Practice Rendering:** Ruthlessly edit your physical and mental space, keeping only what serves your current mission.

The Trap: We confuse editing with aesthetic minimalism or self-deprivation. We hoard things, ideas, and relationships because we think they represent who we are, or who we used to be.

The Way Out: This rule is purely about agility and cognitive load. Carrying excess baggage, whether that is physical clutter on your desk, a toxic relationship you cling to out of habit, or holding onto old, exhausting grudges, requires massive amounts of mental RAM. It slows down your response time to the present moment. Clear it out.

- **Modern Example:** Finally taking the boxes of old, unused gear or mementos from a past relationship to the donation bin. You stop hoarding the physical artifacts of an old identity, freeing up space and making room for the person you are actively choosing to be right now. Clutter is a physical manifestation of indecision.

P15: Question the Default

 **Practice Rendering:** Trust active observation over passive tradition; do what actually works, not what is merely expected.

The Trap: We think this is about being an edgy contrarian or a rebel just for the sake of making noise. We blindly follow the traditions of our company, our family, or our social circle because "that's just how it's done," even when the results are demonstrably toxic or inefficient.

The Way Out: It's actually about ruthless efficiency and honesty. Observe the results. If the "normal" way your industry operates is clearly broken, you must have the courage to discard it without hesitation, regardless of social pressure.

- **Modern Example:** Realizing the mandatory Friday happy hour is just a toxic complaint session that drains your energy. You challenge the social default, risking the mild annoyance of coworkers to reclaim your evening for your family. "Because we've always done it this way" is a dangerous excuse.

Daily Practices

Choose *one* of these practices to execute during your day.

Practice 1: The "Why Am I Eating This?" Drill (Awareness)
For the entirety of today, before you put any food or beverage (other than water) into your mouth, you must pause for three seconds and silently ask: *"Am I consuming this for physical fuel, or am I consuming this to artificially change my emotional state?"*

- *Purpose:* You do not have to aggressively diet today, but you do have to be completely honest with yourself about *why* you are eating. This breaks the powerful autopilot mechanism of emotional eating and consumption.

Practice 2: The 15-Minute Edit (Active) Set a timer for exactly 15 minutes. Pick one specific area of your life that feels heavy, cluttered, or chaotic (your email inbox, your physical desk, your closet, or the apps on your phone's home screen). Ruthlessly delete, throw away, or file anything that does not actively serve your current mission.

- *Purpose:* To prove how quickly you can reclaim massive amounts of mental bandwidth just by removing unnecessary friction and visual clutter from your environment.

Practice 3: The "No" Rep (Social Drill) Identify one incoming request today (an invitation to a meeting you aren't needed in, a request for a favor that drains you, an upsell) and politely but firmly say "No" without offering a massive, groveling excuse.

- *Purpose:* To build the muscle of protecting your time and questioning the default expectation of total compliance.

Evening Anchor: Journal Prompts

Tonight, clear away all distractions. Set a timer for 10 minutes and answer these honestly:

1. Did I consume anything today (food, alcohol, social media, online shopping) specifically to escape an uncomfortable feeling, boredom, or stress?

2. What is one physical item in my home that I am hoarding purely out of guilt or a desperate attachment to a past version of myself?

3. What is one "default" social obligation or habit in my life that I secretly dread, and why haven't I had the courage to edit it out?

4. Who in my life am I "clinging" to out of a fear of loneliness, rather than choosing them out of genuine, reciprocal connection?

5. How can I create more physical or mental "white space" in my schedule tomorrow?

Your Carry Card for Tomorrow

Write these lines on a small piece of paper or an index card. Carry it in your pocket or place it directly on your keyboard for Day 6.

Eat for tomorrow's energy, not today's stress. Clutter is physical indecision. Clear it out. Tradition is not a strategy. Question the default.

Close: You are getting lighter. By editing your physical space, questioning societal expectations, and unmasking your deepest comfort habits, you are building the agility required for true discipline. You are dropping the rocks from your backpack. But there is one final, heavy truth we must confront before this retreat ends.

Tomorrow, we face the ticking clock. We face our own mortality, the urgency of the present moment, and the harsh, undeniable reality that our time to execute is rapidly running out. Get some sleep.

DAY 6:

THE TICKING CLOCK, ESSENTIALS, AND GRACE

For five days, you have been fighting. You have fought your own ego, your deepest desires for comfort, your deeply ingrained habits, and your physical environment. You have been building a fortress.

Today, the tone shifts. Today, you lay down your weapons and step outside the fortress to look at the horizon.

When Musashi wrote the *Dokkōdō*, he was actively dying. He knew his time was rapidly expiring. He could not take his swords with him. Most modern people spend their entire lives frantically avoiding the thought of death, terrified of their own mortality. We act as if we have an infinite amount of time to fix our relationships, launch our projects, and become the people we want to be. But when you refuse to look at the ticking clock, you end up wasting your precious, finite hours on the trivial, the petty, and the purely logistical. You hoard money out of a deep-seated fear of an uncontrollable future, completely bankrupting the time you have today. You buy endless amounts of "gear" to prepare for hobbies you never actually start.

Contemplating your mortality is not morbid or depressing. It is deeply, profoundly comforting. It is the ultimate filter. When you realize the clock is ticking, the heavy, exhausting burden of trying to do *everything* perfectly completely vanishes. You only have to do what is essential. You learn to build internal resilience instead of hoarding external resources, and you learn to value deep presence over endless planning.

Today is about a gentle, quiet acceptance of time.

Track A: Nate's Morning

It was Saturday morning. Nate woke up at 7:00 AM.

Usually, Saturdays were a source of profound, low-grade anxiety for him. He suffered from "Optimization Disease." He viewed the weekend as a frenzied, desperate race to catch up on everything he had failed to do during the week. He would spend his Saturday mornings obsessively mapping out chores, creating complex, exhausting itineraries for family outings, and browsing Amazon for expensive backyard equipment, convinced that buying a $500 playset would somehow automatically make him a "good dad" and guarantee perfect, photogenic memories.

He sat down at the kitchen table with his laptop, ready to execute his usual Saturday planning stress. The kids were playing on the rug in the living room, building a wildly structurally unsound fort out of sofa cushions.

Nate opened his Morning Anchor. He read Precept 16: *Master a few essential tools or skills rather than hoarding gear and superficial knowledge.* Then, he read Precept 17: *Accept your mortality to live with urgency, clarity, and zero hesitation.*

Nate stopped typing. He looked away from the glowing screen and watched his five-year-old daughter laugh as the cushion fort collapsed around her.

Your time is expiring right now, the precept warned. *Act accordingly.*

The math hit him with a quiet, breath-stealing clarity. His daughter was five. If she left for college at eighteen, he had exactly thirteen summers left where she lived under his roof. Thirteen. The number wasn't abstract; it was finite, countable, and rapidly shrinking. Every weekend he spent stressed out about optimizing their time was a weekend completely lost.

He looked down at his laptop screen. He had an Amazon tab open, researching the best, most highly-reviewed, expensive camping gear for a hypothetical family trip he had been putting off for a year. He was hoarding gear (Precept 16) instead of just taking action, hoping the equipment would do the heavy lifting of parenting for him.

Nate slowly closed the laptop. The sudden urge to "optimize" the weekend completely evaporated. The anxiety about being perfectly productive faded into a gentle, settling peace. He didn't need to buy a $500 playset. He didn't need to curate a perfect, Instagram-worthy family outing to a museum. Those were just distractions from the actual work of being present.

The essential thing was right in front of him.

Nate stood up from the table. He walked into the living room, grabbed a throw pillow, and dropped directly onto the floor next to the collapsed fort.

"Alright," Nate said, smiling as his kids immediately piled on top of him. "Let's rebuild this thing. But this time, we need a drawbridge."

He didn't check his phone or open his laptop for the next three hours. It wasn't an explosive, dramatic victory of discipline. It was just a quiet, profound return to what was essential, fueled by the gentle acceptance that this exact season of his life was incredibly fleeting.

Track B: Cole's Morning

Saturday was Cole's designated day to handle his personal logistics.

By 0900, he was sitting at his pristine desk, rigorously reviewing his financial portfolios, his retirement projections, and his insurance policies. Cole was a master at hoarding resources (Precept 18). Since his divorce, he had become obsessed with financial security. He poured every spare dollar into investments, terrified of a future where he might be vulnerable, sick, or reliant on anyone else. He felt secure only when the numbers on the screen went up.

His phone rang. It was the assisted living facility where his seventy-two-year-old father lived, just a thirty-minute drive away. It wasn't an emergency, just a routine check-in from a nurse regarding a minor change in his father's blood pressure medication.

"He's doing okay, Mr. Davis," the nurse said gently. "But he's definitely slowing down this month. He sleeps a lot more. You should come by if you have the time this weekend."

Cole hung up the phone. A heavy, cold dread settled in his chest.

Usually, when Cole visited his father, he engaged in the "logistics of avoidance." He treated the visit like a military inspection. He would march in, check the room temperature, inspect the cleanliness of the bathroom, restock the mini-fridge with aggressive efficiency, and leave an hour later without having a real conversation. Cole used extreme logistical control to completely avoid the terrifying emotional reality that his father was dying. He was building financial hoards instead of building emotional resilience.

Cole realized, with a sickening drop in his stomach, that he was aggressively hoarding money for a hypothetical future that wasn't guaranteed, while actively bankrupting the very real, very limited time he had left with his father today.

Cole shut down the computer. He didn't put on his usual armor of a stiff polo shirt and a watch. He put on a comfortable sweater, drove to his favorite, expensive local deli, and bought two massive, heavily-stacked pastrami sandwiches, spending the money he usually hoarded so carefully.

When he walked into the assisted living room, the smell of sterile cleaners hit him. His father was sitting in an armchair by the window, looking alarmingly frail, watching the traffic below.

The old Cole would have immediately started adjusting the blinds and asking about the medication schedule.

Today, Cole pulled up a chair directly across from his father. He handed him the paper-wrapped sandwich.

"I brought lunch, Dad," Cole said softly.

His father looked up, surprised by the break in routine, and took the sandwich. "Pastrami. You shouldn't be spending your money on this, Cole."

"The money is fine," Cole said, his voice thick with uncharacteristic emotion. He sat back, entirely letting go of the desperate urge to fix or manage the room. "I just wanted to sit with you. Tell me about the car you bought when you first met Mom."

His father's eyes lit up, the fatigue temporarily fading as he launched into the story. Cole just sat there and listened. He didn't look at his watch. He accepted the reality of his father's fading health not with rigid denial or logistical panic, but with a deep, open, and gentle grace. He was finally living with urgency.

The 3 Precepts of the Day

P16: Master the Essentials

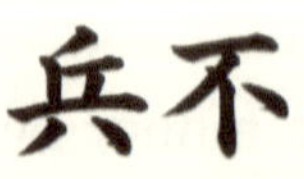

Practice Rendering: Master a few essential tools or skills rather than hoarding gear and superficial knowledge.

The Trap: We get caught in a modern trap called "gear acquisition syndrome," genuinely believing that buying the perfect leather notebook, downloading a complex new productivity app, or buying expensive athletic equipment is the exact same thing as actually doing the hard work. We use buying things as a substitute for skill.

The Way Out: Strip away the excess. Commit to mastering the basic, unglamorous fundamentals of your craft, your fitness, or your relationships using only the absolute minimum required tools.

- **Modern Example:** Realizing you are using app-switching and constant planning as a form of procrastination. You delete three different complex, expensive productivity platforms from your phone and go back to a simple, cheap pen and a legal pad to aggressively manage your top three daily tasks. Amateurs buy equipment; professionals buy time through mastery.

P17: Live with Urgency

 **Practice Rendering:** Accept your mortality to live with urgency, clarity, and zero hesitation.

The Trap: We think contemplating death is morbid, depressing, or a fast track to nihilism. We live as if we have an infinite number of tomorrows to fix our lives, apologize, or start our projects.

The Way Out: Mortality is the ultimate prioritizing tool. If you truly internalize that your time is strictly limited, holding onto petty arguments, scrolling for three hours, and procrastinating your presence suddenly become completely absurd. It forces you to focus only on what is essential.

- **Modern Example:** Recognizing your aging parent is slowing down. Instead of waiting for a "better time" or treating visits purely as logistical chores, you drive over, put your phone away, and ask the deep, meaningful questions you've been putting off for a decade. Your time is expiring right now. Act accordingly.

P18: Build Resilience, Not Hoards

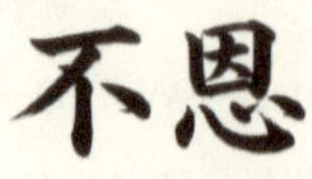 **Practice Rendering:** Build resilience and adaptability for the future instead of anxiously hoarding resources out of fear.

The Trap: We mistakenly think this means you shouldn't save for retirement, buy insurance, or plan ahead. The trap is letting crippling financial anxiety or a scarcity mindset paralyze your current life, turning you into a miserable miser who avoids connection because you are terrified of losing what you have.

The Way Out: True security comes from your internal capability to handle chaos, adapt, and earn, not just a massive, untouchable bank balance. Invest in your skills and your relationships, not just your portfolio.

- **Modern Example:** Recognizing that your obsession with aggressively saving money is rooted in trauma, you intentionally loosen your iron grip on the family budget to fund a spontaneous weekend trip with your kids, realizing that shared memories are a far better investment right now than an extra fraction of a percent in your portfolio.

Daily Practices

Choose *one* of these practices to execute during your day.

Practice 1: The "Last Time" Meditation (Mental Drill) Pick one completely mundane activity you do today (drinking a cup of coffee, driving to the store, or saying goodbye to a family member). As you do it, imagine, vividly and gently, that this is the absolute last time in your entire life you will ever get to do this specific thing. Notice how your attention sharpens, how the colors seem brighter, and how the annoyance fades into profound gratitude.

- *Purpose:* To use mortality not to generate fear, but to instantly generate presence and strip away trivial complaints.

Practice 2: The "Enough" Audit (Active) Open your closet, your garage, or your digital workspace. Identify three specific items, tools, or subscriptions you bought under the delusion that they would make you "better" or "more productive," but that you haven't touched in three months. Cancel them or put them in a donation box.

- *Purpose:* To confront your habit of hoarding gear, realizing that you already possess the essential tools required to do the work.

Practice 3: The Micro-Risk (Active) Do one thing today that feels slightly financially or emotionally risky, simply to prove you won't die. Over-tip a barista, give away a piece of gear you like, or initiate a vulnerable conversation you've been avoiding.

- *Purpose:* To actively break the grip of the hoarding mindset and prove your own resilience.

Evening Anchor: Journal Prompts

Tonight, clear away all distractions. Set a timer for 10 minutes and answer these honestly:

1. If I knew I only had one year left to live, what is the very first project, argument, or anxiety I would immediately drop from my life?

2. What "gear" or tools am I currently hoarding as an excuse to avoid actually starting the hard work of mastery?

3. In what ways am I letting a deep fear of the future prevent me from actually enjoying and participating in my life today?

4. Who in my life needs my pure, unhurried presence right now, rather than my logistical help or my money?

5. How does remembering my own mortality actually make me feel more free?

Your Carry Card for Tomorrow

Write these lines on a small piece of paper or an index card. Carry it in your pocket or place it directly on your keyboard for Day 7.

Your time is expiring right now. Act accordingly. Amateurs buy equipment. Professionals buy time through mastery. True security is knowing you can handle whatever happens.

Close: You have looked at the hardest truth. You have looked at the ticking clock, and instead of panicking, you let it clarify your vision. The heavy burden of needing to do everything perfectly has been lifted. You only have to do what matters. Tomorrow is Day 7. The final day.

Tomorrow, we integrate everything we've learned, take uncompromising responsibility, and learn the most critical skill of all: how to return to the path after you inevitably fail. Get some sleep.

DAY 7:

INTEGRATION, INTEGRITY, AND THE RETURN

This is the final day of the retreat. But the true test of this operating system is not what happens today. The true test is what happens on Day 8, when the retreat is officially over, the novelty has completely worn off, and your messy, demanding life continues without a guide.

Many people treat discipline like a fragile, incredibly delicate glass sculpture. They build a "perfect streak" of early mornings, clean eating, and meditation. But the moment they oversleep, eat a donut, or lose their temper, the glass shatters into a thousand pieces. They tell themselves, *Well, I ruined the streak. I failed. I might as well quit completely, binge on bad habits, and start over next month.* That is ego talking. It is an ego that demands unbroken perfection in order to feel worthy.

Today, we violently destroy that fragility. Today is about integration. We are going to look at the uncompromising nature of personal responsibility, the unglamorous reality of modern integrity, and the ultimate secret to lifelong discipline: the speed of your return. You will learn that the path is not a straight, unbroken line. The path is built purely through the act of returning to it, over and over again, after you stray.

Track A: Nate's Morning

It was Sunday morning. Nate was in the garage, tasked with a chore he had been aggressively putting off for a month: building a large, heavy, complex wooden shelving unit for Claire's gardening supplies.

He was tired. The retreat had demanded a lot of cognitive energy this week. As he knelt on the cold concrete, trying to decipher the terrible, wordless instruction manual, his five-year-old daughter, Maya, ran into the garage. She was singing loudly, twirling a plastic wand, and repeatedly bumping into Nate's legs.

"Maya, please, Daddy needs to focus," Nate said, his voice tight with rising frustration.

He balanced a heavy wooden plank on his knee, trying to align the final screws. Maya bumped his shoulder, and the plank slipped, crashing down, painfully clipping Nate's shin, and slamming onto the concrete floor, splintering the corner of the expensive wood.

A massive, hot wave of pure anger surged up Nate's throat.

His immediate instinct was to explode. He desperately wanted to yell at Maya to get out of the garage. He wanted to angrily storm into the house, blame Claire for buying a "cheap, impossible-to-build shelf," and declare that the entire Sunday was ruined. He wanted to be a victim of his circumstances.

Then, the final three precepts of his morning reading hit him like a circuit breaker.

Precept 19: *Take absolute, uncompromising responsibility for your own actions.* Precept 21: *Commit unconditionally to your daily practice, knowing the path is built through continuous, unglamorous return.*

Nate closed his eyes. He stopped the victim narrative in its tracks. *I am a grown man,* he thought. *I am responsible for securing the plank. I am responsible for my own temper. Maya is just being a five-year-old. I am not a victim.*

He took a slow, deep breath, letting the red-hot anger dissolve into the cold air of the garage.

"It's okay, sweetie," Nate said calmly, rubbing his shin. "Can you go play in the grass for a few minutes while I finish this up?"

Maya skipped away, unbothered. Nate looked down at the splintered wood. The old Nate would have thrown the screwdriver across the room and quit for the day, deeply ashamed of his failure to stay calm, letting the "broken streak" dictate his entire afternoon. The new Nate realized that feeling the anger wasn't the failure; letting it drive the car was.

He had strayed from his intention. He had felt the rage. But the discipline wasn't in being perfect. The discipline was entirely in how fast he returned to the standard.

He picked up the screwdriver. He aligned the heavy plank. He tightened the screws and finished the shelf.

Later that afternoon, sitting at the kitchen island, Nate pulled out a blank index card. It was time for his final retreat exercise. He reviewed the 21 precepts he had studied all week. He didn't need to memorize all twenty-one perfectly. He needed a shorthand, a personal code he could carry into the chaos of Monday morning. He grabbed a pen and began to write his own "Dokkōdō-Lite," distilling the massive philosophy into a handful of unbreakable, foundational rules for his specific life as a father and a professional. He was finally anchored.

Track B: Cole's Morning

Sunday was transition day for Cole. At 1400 hours, he was scheduled to drive to his ex-wife's house to drop off the teenagers, officially ending his custody weekend.

At 1000 hours, while Cole was meticulously cleaning his kitchen, his phone buzzed. It was a text from his ex-wife, Sarah.

I am so sorry, Cole. An emergency pipe burst at the bakery, and I had to come in to manage the plumbers. It's a total disaster here. I won't be home until at least 1900. Can you keep the kids and feed them dinner?

Cole stared at the glowing text message, his jaw muscles instantly clenching.

His Track B schedule was perfectly mapped out. He had planned to drop the kids off at 1400, hit a grueling 90-minute ruck march at the state park by 1500, and spend his Sunday evening quietly reading and preparing for the week ahead in total, uninterrupted solitude. His entire day was built around this rigid transition of responsibility.

The old Cole, the man who used rigid scheduling as emotional armor, would have been furious. He would have viewed Sarah's text as a massive, disrespectful violation of his boundaries and his time. He would have replied with a cold, highly passive-aggressive message about how her "lack of planning" wasn't his emergency. He would have spent the rest of the day silently seething, making the kids deeply uncomfortable in their own home.

He looked at his notebook on the counter.

Precept 19: *Honor the unknown... but take absolute, uncompromising responsibility for your own actions.* Precept 20: *Protect your integrity and core character, even when it costs you comfort, status, or safety.*

Hope was not a strategy. He couldn't magically fix Sarah's plumbing issue by complaining about it. The reality of the board state had permanently changed. The only thing Cole truly controlled was his own integrity as a father. Did his core character demand that he rigidly adhere to a spreadsheet, or did his character demand that he step up, without complaint, when his family system experienced friction?

Integrity wasn't about looking tough in a gym. It was about actually being a reliable, load-bearing pillar in a storm.

Cole didn't hesitate. He deleted the frustrated response he had started typing in his head.

Absolutely not a problem, Cole texted back quickly. *Focus on the bakery. I'll make steaks tonight and drop them off at 1930. Let me know if you need anything else.*

He put the phone down. He didn't feel the familiar, bitter resentment of being "taken advantage of." He simply felt the quiet, deeply satisfying weight of true responsibility. He had surrendered the outcome, accepted the reality, and protected his character.

That evening, after adjusting his plans, grilling dinner, and finally dropping the kids off, Cole returned to his quiet, empty house. He walked into his den and sat down at his desk.

He realized that his massive, color-coded spreadsheet, the rigid Track B schedule he had clung to all week, was just a training wheel. It was a cast for a broken bone. But the bone had healed. He didn't need to micromanage every single minute of his existence to feel secure anymore. He just needed a compass.

Cole opened his heavy leather journal. He looked at the 21 precepts. Slowly, methodically, he began to draft his own 7-rule code. He pared away the excess, keeping only the raw, essential principles that would govern how he operated in his business, in his gym, and, most importantly, with his children. He closed the book, the retreat complete, and for the first time in years, he felt completely ready for Monday.

The 3 Precepts of the Day

P19: Take Absolute Responsibility

Practice Rendering: Honor the unknown and respect higher powers, but take absolute, uncompromising responsibility for your own actions.

The Trap: We use bad luck, fate, macroeconomic conditions, or the failures of other people as a comfortable, warm excuse for our own lack of progress. Victimhood feels incredibly safe because it immediately absolves you of the grueling repair work. If it's someone else's fault, you don't have to fix it.

The Way Out: You can pray for smooth sailing or a good economy, but you still have to relentlessly row the boat yourself. Absolute responsibility means owning your response to the chaos, regardless of who caused the chaos.

- **Modern Example:** Your ex-spouse or co-parent experiences an emergency that completely ruins your perfectly planned Sunday schedule. Instead of throwing a passive-aggressive tantrum and acting like a victim, you take immediate ownership of the new reality, adjust the plan without complaint, and handle the friction. Hope is not a strategy.

P20: Protect Your Integrity

Practice Rendering: Protect your integrity and core character, even when it costs you comfort, status, or safety.

The Trap: We think honor is a dramatic, cinematic, battlefield concept reserved for heroes in movies. We assume we will rise to the occasion during a massive crisis, while quietly making a thousand tiny compromises of our integrity every single day to avoid awkward conversations.

The Way Out: Modern honor is incredibly boring, quiet, and unglamorous. It is simply choosing to keep your word, do the hard right thing, and fulfill your duties when it's deeply inconvenient, financially costly, and absolutely no one is watching to give you credit.

- **Modern Example:** Realizing a budgeting mistake you made three weeks ago just cost the company thousands of dollars. Even though you could easily bury the error in a spreadsheet or vaguely shift the blame onto a confusing software update, you choose the sick feeling in your stomach, walk directly into your director's office, and own the mistake entirely. Your reputation is what others think. Your character is what you know.

P21: Return to the Path

Practice Rendering: Commit unconditionally to your daily practice, knowing the path is built through continuous, unglamorous return.

The Trap: We falsely believe that true discipline means an unbroken streak of perfection where you never fail, oversleep, or lose your temper. This is a fragile illusion that causes people to quit entirely on Day 4 when they inevitably mess up. We let the broken streak ruin the whole endeavor.

The Way Out: True discipline is simply a measurement of the speed at which you return to the standard immediately after you inevitably fall short. The master fails more times than the beginner has even tried.

- **Modern Example:** Completely losing your temper at a subordinate or a child, shattering your ideal of being a "stoic, disciplined person." Instead of spiraling into self-hatred, declaring the day a wash, or letting your ego justify the outburst, you take a deep breath, apologize directly, reset your mental posture, and start the practice over in the very next hour. The discipline is in the return.

Daily Practices

Choose *one* of these practices to execute today.

Practice 1: Draft Your "Dokkōdō–Lite" (Active Integration) You cannot carry 21 distinct rules in your working memory during a crisis. Today, you must synthesize the retreat. Review the 21 Precepts. Distill them down into your own personal, 7-rule code. Write them in your own voice, focusing on your specific weaknesses (e.g., "I will not use sugar to solve work stress," or "I will not complain about things I refuse to change"). Write this 7-rule code on a fresh card. This is your new operating system.

- *Purpose:* To shift the philosophy from Musashi's ancient words into your actual, modern life, creating a highly functional shorthand for daily discipline.

Practice 2: The 60-Second Return (Mental Drill) Think of the specific habit you are most likely to break tomorrow (hitting snooze, scrolling social media, snapping at your partner). Mentally rehearse, in vivid detail, the exact moment you fail. Then, visualize yourself pausing, dropping the guilt instantly, and returning to the correct behavior within 60 seconds without a massive internal monologue.

- *Purpose:* To pre-program your brain's recovery sequence, completely removing the heavy, dramatic "failure spiral" when you inevitably mess up.

Practice 3: The Ownership Audit (Active) Find one situation in your life right now where you are actively blaming someone else (a boss, a spouse, the economy). Write down exactly what *you* did to contribute to the situation, or exactly what *you* are failing to do to fix it.

. *Purpose:* To destroy the victim narrative and reclaim your agency.

Evening Anchor: Journal Prompts

Tonight, as the retreat concludes, clear away all distractions. Set a timer for 15 minutes and answer these honestly:

1. Where in my life am I still playing the victim, blaming my circumstances or other people instead of taking absolute responsibility for my own response?

2. Did I make any small compromises in my integrity this week just to avoid an uncomfortable conversation or save face?

3. When I inevitably "fall off the path" next week, what is my exact, step-by-step protocol for returning without self-hatred?

4. Looking back at the last seven days, which of the two Tracks (Nate's flexibility or Cole's structure) actually suits my real life better, and how will I adapt it moving forward?

5. What are the 7 core rules of my new "Dokkōdō-Lite"?

The Repeat Plan

Write this on your final carry card and keep it visible.

The retreat is never over. It is only repeated.

The Weekly Reset: Every Sunday evening, read your personal 7-rule "Dokkōdō-Lite" code. Edit it if your life season has changed. **The Quarterly Return:** Once a quarter, when the noise gets too loud, your ego gets too heavy, and you find yourself constantly complaining, return to Day 1 of this book. Run the 7-day Reigandō Reset again. Choose your Track. Clean out the mud. Rebuild the anchor.

Final Close: The cave wasn't magic. It was just quiet. And now, you know how to build that quiet wherever you go. You have the tools to shrink your ego, accept reality, edit the noise, and act on intention regardless of the weather. You will stumble. You will stray. But you now know the secret: the path is not about perfection. The path is the return.

Step out of the cave. Get to work.

Appendix:

The Retreat Tools

This appendix contains the pure, functional tools you need to execute the Reigandō Reset. Do not just read this book and put it on a shelf to gather dust alongside other theoretical self-improvement manuals; use it as a workbench.

The philosophy of Musashi is entirely useless if it remains abstract. Copy these templates into your own notebook, physically write out the carry cards by hand, and refer heavily back to the FAQ when your ego inevitably tries to convince you to quit on Day 3. Print these pages. Treat this physical stack of paper as your daily operating manual for the next seven days.

1. Retreat Checklist: "Set Your Cave"

Complete this checklist on **Setup Night** (the evening before Day 1). Do not skip this phase. Your success or failure on this retreat will largely be determined by the logistical decisions you make the night before you begin.

- **Commit to a Track:** Get a physical piece of paper. Write down "Track A" (Flexible) or "Track B" (Structured) in large letters and place it on your nightstand or tape it to your bathroom mirror. Make the decision real and visible.

  - *Crucial Warning:* Do not choose the track you *wish* you had the life for. Ego will try to trick you here. If you have a newborn or unpredictable shift work, choose Track A. If you have total calendar autonomy, choose Track B. Choose the one that fits tomorrow's raw reality.

- **Stage Your Friction:** Willpower is a rapidly depleting resource, and it is at its lowest point at 5:30 AM. Do not waste cognitive energy on logistics when you are tired.

  - *If Track A:* Decide exactly *where* your morning anchor will happen (e.g., sitting in your parked car before entering the office, or at the kitchen counter before the kids wake up). Claim the physical space now.

  - *If Track B:* Set your alarm, lay out your workout clothes and shoes, and physically plug your phone into a wall outlet in an entirely separate room so you cannot reach it from the bed.

- **Clear the Deck:** Look closely at your calendar for the next seven days. Find one thing, a non-essential meeting, a social obligation you only agreed to out of guilt, or a nightly television habit, and ruthlessly cancel it. Buy yourself back at least one hour of daily margin. You will need that space to process the retreat.

- **Prepare Your Tools:** Have a dedicated physical notebook, a reliable pen, and exactly 7 blank index cards (or small pieces of paper) ready and stacked on your desk or nightstand. Do not do this retreat digitally on your phone; the screen is a portal to distraction.

2. Schedule Templates

Track A: The Flexible Retreat (Anchored Blocks)

Designed for unpredictable schedules, parents of young children, first responders, and shift workers.

Track A relies on the understanding that "flexible" does not mean "optional." You cannot control when your windows of time will open, but you must be violently protective of them when they do.

- Morning Anchor (10-25 min): * *When:* The very first window of quiet you get, even if it's brief or suboptimal.

  - *Action:* Read the daily precepts + execute the daily practice. If you are interrupted by a crying child or an urgent call, pause without anger, handle the chaos, and return to the anchor.

- Midday Anchor (5-15 min): * *When:* During a lunch break, a commute, or immediately following a highly stressful event.

  - *Action:* Execute a tactical reset drill (e.g., Urge Surfing, the "What Is" Drill). This acts as a psychological circuit breaker to stop the negative momentum of the morning from bleeding into your afternoon.

- Evening Anchor (10-25 min): * *When:* When the dust finally settles for the day, right before you go to sleep.

    ○ *Action:* Complete the daily journal prompts + physically write out tomorrow's Carry Card. Place it on your keyboard, your dashboard, or your bathroom mirror so it is the first thing you see tomorrow. Do not skip this; it seals the day.

Track B: The Structured Retreat (Fixed Schedule)

Designed for empty-nesters, single professionals, or those with high calendar autonomy who require a rigid reset to break bad habits.

Track B relies on holding a hard, uncompromising line against your own excuses. You must defend these time blocks as if your life depends on them.

- 0500 – Wake & Silence Walk: 15 minutes moving outside immediately after waking. No inputs allowed (no phone, no music, no podcasts). Just you, the morning air, and the uncomfortable reality of your own unedited thoughts.

- 0600 – Reading Block: Study the day's precepts with a pen in hand. Mark what challenges you.

- 0630 – Practice Block: Execute the daily physical or mental drill with absolute focus.

- 0800 to 1700 – Execution: Distraction-free, uncompromising execution of your daily professional or personal duties.

- 1200 – Midday Reset: A strict 10-minute disconnection block. Step away from your desk. Do not look at any screens. Close your eyes and lower your heart rate.

- 2000 – Evening Reflection: Complete the daily journal prompts + write out tomorrow's Carry Card. Once this is finished, the workday is officially closed.

3. The 7-Day Journal Templates

Set a timer for 10-15 minutes each night. Answer the prompts rapidly and honestly. Do not edit yourself, and do not perform for an imaginary audience. No one is reading this but you. The value is in the friction of the truth. Write your answers by hand. The physical act of writing forces you to slow down and prevents you from tabbing over to a distraction.

Day 1: Reality, Not Fantasy *Focus: Exposing the gap between what you demand from life and what is actually happening.*

1. Where did I waste valuable cognitive energy today aggressively arguing with reality instead of just dealing with the facts on the ground?

2. When the day got stressful or boring, what was my default "escape hatch" (social media, junk food, snapping in anger, zoning out), and what specific emotional discomfort was I trying to run away from?

3. Did I let a temporary, passing mood dictate how I treated someone important to me today?

4. If I had operated entirely on my core *intentions* today instead of my fleeting impulses, what specific moments or interactions would have looked radically different?

5. Where can I realistically expect reality to be messy or difficult tomorrow, and how will I prepare my mind to accept it?

Day 2: Desire and Dopamine *Focus: Identifying how your ego and your desperation for specific outcomes make you fragile.*

1. In what highly specific area of my life am I completely, hopelessly enslaved by the outcome (a promotion, a scale weight, a specific person's approval)?

2. If I knew with 100% certainty I would fail at that goal, would the daily effort of pursuing it still be worth doing? Why or why not?

3. Did my fragile ego cause completely unnecessary friction or drama for someone else today?

4. What past mistake am I continuing to pay daily emotional "interest" on, and what is the exact, unvarnished lesson I need to extract so I can drop it forever?

5. How specifically can I "shrink the ego" tomorrow morning?

Day 3: Comparison, Complaining, and the Noise *Focus: Plugging the massive energy leaks caused by looking at other people's lives and whining about your own.*

1. Who specifically did I compare myself to today, and what deep, underlying insecurity did that brief comparison trigger in me?

2. What is one specific "season" or phase of my life that is currently ending, and how am I stubbornly fighting that transition instead of accepting it gracefully?

3. What was the absolute most useless, energy-draining complaint that came out of my mouth today?

4. If I took all the mental energy I wasted complaining and comparing today and strictly applied it to a personal goal, what could I have accomplished?

5. Where specifically do I need to strictly keep my eyes in my own boat tomorrow?

Day 4: Status, Environment, and the Core *Focus: Becoming completely environmentally bulletproof and protecting your foundations from the high of infatuation.*

1. What specific tool, environment, or "perfect condition" am I currently using as a comfortable excuse for my lack of progress?

2. How did I react the last time my environment was chaotic or suboptimal? Did I adapt and execute, or did I whine and shut down?

3. Where in my life am I currently infatuated (with a new idea, a new purchase, or a new person), and is that infatuation causing me to neglect my foundational duties?

4. Did I make any decisions today purely to look important or maintain status in front of other people?

5. How can I practice anchoring internally tomorrow when the external noise starts?

Day 5: Consumption, Clutter, and the Default *Focus: Ruthlessly editing your physical space and challenging the broken social norms of your environment.*

1. Did I consume anything today (food, alcohol, social media) specifically to escape an uncomfortable feeling, boredom, or stress?

2. What is one physical item in my home that I am hoarding purely out of guilt or an attachment to a past version of myself?

3. What is one "default" social obligation or habit in my life that I secretly dread, and why haven't I had the courage to edit it out?

4. Who in my life am I "clinging" to out of a fear of loneliness, rather than choosing them out of genuine connection?

5. How can I create more physical or mental "white space" in my schedule tomorrow?

Day 6: The Ticking Clock, Essentials, and Grace *Focus: Using the undeniable reality of your own mortality to clarify what actually matters right now.*

1. If I knew I only had one year left to live, what is the very first project, argument, or anxiety I would immediately drop from my life?

2. What "gear" or tools am I currently hoarding as an excuse to avoid actually starting the hard work of mastery?

3. In what ways am I letting a deep, paralyzing fear of the future prevent me from actually enjoying and participating in my life today?

4. Who in my life needs my pure, unhurried presence right now, rather than my logistical help or my money?

5. How does remembering my own mortality actually make me feel more free?

Day 7: Integration, Integrity, and The Return *Focus: Distilling the retreat into a repeatable operating system and mastering the speed of your recovery.*

1. Where in my life am I still playing the victim, blaming my circumstances or other people instead of taking absolute responsibility for my own response?

2. Did I make any small compromises in my integrity this week just to avoid an uncomfortable conversation or save face?

3. When I inevitably "fall off the path" next week, what is my exact, step-by-step protocol for returning without self-hatred?

4. Looking back at the last seven days, which of the two Tracks (Nate's flexibility or Cole's structure) actually suits my real life better, and how will I adapt it moving forward?

5. What are the 7 core rules of my new "Dokkōdō-Lite"?

4. Carry Cards

Write the bolded lines onto a physical index card each night. Do not use a digital notes app. Keep the card in your pocket, on your dashboard, or physically resting on your keyboard the following day. It is designed to act as a physical tripwire against your worst habits.

Day 1 Carry Card

- Stop arguing with what is. Deal with what is.

- Notice the escape hatch.

. Mood is weather. Intention is the compass.

Day 2 Carry Card

. You are not the main character.

. Control the effort. Surrender the result.

. Extract the lesson. Burn the regret.

Day 3 Carry Card

. Comparison is a thief. Keep your eyes in your own boat.

. Everything has a season. Let it go gracefully.

. If you can fix it, fix it. If you can't, complaining is noise.

Day 4 Carry Card

. Enjoy the fire, but don't let it burn down the house.

. The perfect setup is a myth. Use what is in front of you.

. Your environment does not dictate your focus. You do.

Day 5 Carry Card

. Eat for tomorrow's energy, not today's stress.

. Clutter is physical indecision. Clear it out.

. Tradition is not a strategy. Question the default.

Day 6 Carry Card

. Your time is expiring right now. Act accordingly.

. Amateurs buy equipment. Professionals buy time through mastery.

- True security is knowing you can handle whatever happens.

Day 7 Carry Card

- Your reputation is what others think. Your character is what you know.

- Hope is not a strategy. You must do the work yourself.

- You will stray. The discipline is in the return.

5. FAQ + Misreads

When applying ancient, austere philosophy to modern, chaotic life, it is incredibly easy for your ego to weaponize the rules against yourself. Watch out for these common, destructive misreads of the text.

Misread #1: "Detachment means I should be cold and uncaring." Detachment does not equal emotional numbness. Musashi did not teach apathy. Apathy is the coward's way out. True detachment takes immense courage because it means you care deeply and passionately about the *effort* you put into a relationship, a job, or a goal, but you simultaneously accept that you cannot control the final *result*. If you use detachment as an excuse to freeze out your spouse during an argument, ignore your kids, or stop trying at work to protect yourself from failure, you aren't being disciplined; you are just being afraid of getting hurt.

Misread #2: "Solitude means I need to isolate myself from people." You do not have a cave, and you shouldn't try to artificially build one by abandoning your familial or professional responsibilities. Modern solitude is not about physical isolation; it is entirely about *internal quiet*. It is the highly trained ability to sit in a chaotic, loud room and maintain your own internal gravity without being helplessly pulled into everyone else's drama and anxiety. True, functional solitude makes you *better* and more present for your family, not absent from them.

Misread #3: "Discipline means punishing myself." Discipline is not self-flagellation. If you treat this retreat as a brutal way to punish yourself for your past mistakes, your waistline, or your lack of focus, you will exhaust yourself and quit by Day 3. Discipline is simply the strategic, calm removal of friction between where you currently are and where you intend to be. It is an act of deep self-respect, not self-hatred. If your daily routine makes you brittle, deeply angry, and miserable to be around, your routine is fundamentally broken and must be edited.

How to Restart After Breaking the Rules: Let us be clear: you will break the rules. You will snap at your kids, eat the donut, mindlessly scroll for two hours, and feel the bitter sting of comparison. Perfection is an illusion. When you inevitably fall short, follow the **60-Second Return Protocol:**

1. **Acknowledge it bluntly:** Stop what you are doing and state the fact out loud. *"I failed the standard just now. I lost my temper."* Do not sugarcoat it.

2. **Drop the ego:** Do not wallow in guilt. Guilt feels like penance, but it is just your ego throwing a pity party. Burn the regret immediately.

3. **Execute the Return:** Do not say "the day is ruined, I'll start again tomorrow." Start again in the very next minute. Apologize if necessary, put the phone down, and reset your posture. The discipline is measured entirely by the speed of the return. Now, step out of the cave. Your retreat begins tomorrow.

PRACTICE RENDERINGS:

P1–P21

Document Purpose:

The foundational plain-English translations of Musashi's 21 precepts for the *Dokkōdō: The Reigandō Reset* retreat.

Disclaimer:

Different translations of the historical Dokkōdō vary significantly in their wording. The rules below are Practice Renderings (Plain-English), they are unique phrasing designed strictly for modern clarity and daily application, not as canonical historical text.

P1: Accept Reality

Practice Rendering: Acknowledge reality exactly as it presents itself, without demanding it be different before you act.

What People Get Wrong: They think this means passive surrender, giving up, or pretending a bad situation is actually good. In truth, it means stopping the exhausting, invisible mental argument with reality ("This shouldn't be happening," "It's not fair," "I didn't plan for this"). That internal argument drains the exact cognitive energy you need to actually solve the problem. Acceptance is the prerequisite for immediate, effective action.

- **Nate-style Example:** His toddler dumps a bowl of sticky oatmeal directly onto his open laptop keyboard ten minutes before a major team sync. Instead of spiraling into a victim narrative of "Why does this always happen to me when I'm trying to work?", he immediately bypasses the frustration, grabs a towel, wipes the damage, logs in from his phone, and handles the meeting.

- **Cole-style Example:** A key supplier abruptly backs out of a contract, completely ruining a quarter that Cole spent six months perfectly planning. Instead of wasting an hour pacing his office and raging at the supplier's incompetence, Cole immediately accepts the new board state, opens his contingency file, and starts dialing his secondary backups before his competitors do.

Carry-Card Line: Stop arguing with what is. Deal with what is.

P2: Drop the Chase for Comfort

Practice Rendering: Stop chasing temporary dopamine hits to escape the discomfort of the present moment.

What People Get Wrong: They assume this means you must live like an ascetic monk and never enjoy a cold beer, a good meal, or a movie. It actually means breaking the reflexive habit of using pleasure as a *numbing agent* when you feel stressed, bored, or anxious. When comfort is used as an escape hatch from reality, it becomes a cage that keeps you from addressing the actual source of your stress.

- **Nate-style Example:** Catching himself mindlessly opening Instagram for the fourth time in ten minutes while struggling to write a difficult, politically sensitive email. He recognizes the app is just a pacifier for his anxiety, closes it, and moves his phone to another room to create physical friction against the habit.

- **Cole-style Example:** Realizing his nightly ritual of two glasses of expensive bourbon isn't actually a "reward for a hard day's work," but a chemical crutch he uses to avoid sitting in the uncomfortable, echoing quiet of an empty house. He chooses to pour a glass of water and sit with the silence instead.

Carry-Card Line: Notice when you are using pleasure as an escape hatch.

P3: Act on Intention, Not Mood

Practice Rendering: Base your actions on clear, decided intention, not fluctuating moods or half-hearted impulses.

What People Get Wrong: They think this requires burying your emotions or pretending you are a robot. It actually means recognizing your emotions, acknowledging that you feel furious, exhausted, or unmotivated, but refusing to let those temporary biological states drive the car. Moods are just the weather; your intentions are the map. You don't cancel a vital trip just because it's raining; you just put on a heavier coat.

- **Nate-style Example:** Feeling entirely physically drained and mentally foggy at 5:30 PM after a grueling workday, but actively choosing to sit on the floor and build Legos for ten uninterrupted minutes because his core intention is connection with his kids, regardless of his current energy level.

- **Cole-style Example:** Feeling a sudden, hot flash of anger when his teenage son rolls his eyes and catches an attitude. Instead of his usual barking, ego-driven reprimand, Cole takes a deep breath, remembers his intention to build a resilient relationship, and chooses a measured, calm response.

Carry-Card Line: Your mood is a weather report, not a compass.

P4: Shrink the Ego, Expand the View

Practice Rendering: Shrink your ego and expand your awareness of the people and systems around you.

What People Get Wrong: They read Musashi's original "think lightly of yourself" as a mandate for self-deprecation, low self-esteem, or letting people walk all over you. It actually means taking yourself less seriously so you can stop obsessing over your own image and pay better attention to the room. Ego acts like a blinder; shrinking it gives you peripheral vision.

- **Nate-style Example:** Realizing halfway through a meeting that he's dominating the conversation just to sound like the smartest guy in the room and secure his status. He intentionally steps back, shuts his mouth, and directly asks a quiet junior designer for their input, giving them the floor.

- **Cole-style Example:** Recognizing that his obsession with maintaining his own rigorous, "perfect" weekend schedule is actively making his daughter's time with him stressful and rigid. He chooses to bend his monumental routine to accommodate a spontaneous trip she wants to take.

Carry-Card Line: You are not the main character of everyone else's day.

P5: Detach from the Outcome

Practice Rendering: Pursue your goals fiercely, without becoming emotionally enslaved by the outcome.

What People Get Wrong: They mistake detachment for apathy ("Who cares what happens?"). True detachment takes immense vulnerability, because it means caring deeply about the *effort*, investing heavily in the preparation, while simultaneously accepting that the universe (or the market, or the boss) has absolute veto power over the *result*.

- **Nate-style Example:** Pitching a new product feature he poured his heart into for weeks. When the leadership team bluntly rejects it for budget reasons, he takes the feedback, extracts the necessary data, and closes his laptop without taking the rejection as a personal insult to his worth.

- **Cole-style Example:** Training with brutal consistency for months to hit a specific 405-pound deadlift PR. He steps up to the bar, misses the lift entirely, and calmly strips the weights and racks the bar without throwing a tantrum, kicking a chalk bucket, or beating himself up.

Carry-Card Line: Control the effort. Surrender the result.

P6: Drop the Weight of Regret

Practice Rendering: Extract the operational lesson from past mistakes and immediately drop the emotional weight.

What People Get Wrong: They think dropping regret means being a sociopath who never admits fault or feels remorse. But wallowing in guilt is actually a sneaky form of ego, it feels like penance, but it prevents you from taking new action. Refuse to pay daily interest on a debt you've already settled. Guilt is a useful signal for about five minutes; after that, it's just self-indulgent noise.

- **Nate-style Example:** Snapping at his wife in the chaotic morning rush. Instead of feeling guilty all day, avoiding her texts, and acting weirdly distant that evening out of shame, he apologizes directly and plainly at noon, extracting the lesson and resetting their day.

- **Cole-style Example:** Looking at the numbers and realizing he explicitly hired the wrong project manager six months ago despite warnings. He doesn't wallow in "I should have known better" or sink into a sunk-cost fallacy; he builds a clean transition plan and makes the cut professionally and calmly.

Carry-Card Line: Extract the lesson. Burn the regret.

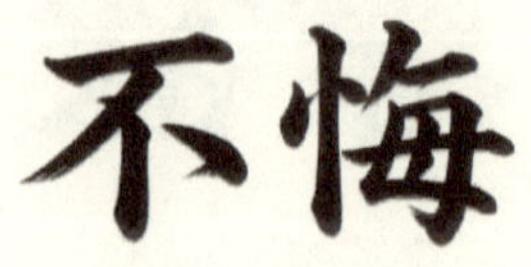

P7: Kill Comparison

Practice Rendering: Recognize that comparing your path to another's wastes the exact energy needed to build your own.

What People Get Wrong: They think jealousy is just about coveting money, cars, or status. More often, modern comparison is being secretly jealous of someone else's apparent ease, their free time, or their lack of friction. We compare our gritty, unedited reality to someone else's curated highlight reel.

- **Nate-style Example:** Scrolling LinkedIn on the couch and seeing a college friend sell a startup for millions. He feels an immediate, sinking pang of inadequacy and the fear that he is falling behind. He actively catches the thought, closes the app, and grounds himself by focusing on his own kids playing in the living room.

- **Cole-style Example:** Feeling a dark wave of bitterness that his ex-wife's new husband gets to play the "fun, easygoing weekend guy" while Cole has to be the strict, uncool disciplinarian. He lets the bitter narrative die and focuses on the quiet, steady value of being a rock for his teenagers.

Carry-Card Line: Comparison is a thief. Keep your eyes in your own boat.

P8: Accept Impermanence

Practice Rendering: Accept that loss and transition are natural, and let go with grace instead of clinging to what was.

What People Get Wrong: They assume this requires a cold, robotic, or uncaring response to loss, grief, or major life changes. It actually means allowing yourself to fully feel the sadness or nostalgia without fighting the undeniable reality that all things, good and bad, eventually end. Suffering comes from the clinging, not the changing.

- **Nate-style Example:** His favorite mentor and work friend abruptly leaves for a rival company. Instead of feeling abandoned, acting resentful, or withdrawing out of self-protection, he takes her to coffee and expresses genuine, unreserved gratitude for the past three years.

- **Cole-style Example:** Realizing his daughter has reached an age where she no longer wants to go on their traditional, early-morning Saturday hikes. He feels the sharp sting of the era passing, accepts that she is growing into her own person, and offers to take her to a late breakfast instead.

Carry-Card Line: Everything has a season. Let it go gracefully.

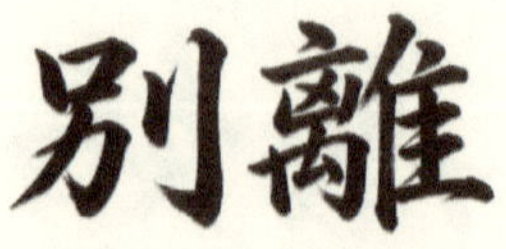

P9: Eliminate Complaints

Practice Rendering: Eliminate whining; it is a passive, toxic refusal to solve the problem in front of you.

What People Get Wrong: They think this rule means they can't ever speak up about injustices, point out flaws, or ask for help. You can and should critique, correct, and strategize. But *complaining* is entirely different, it is repeatedly voicing displeasure to an audience without any intent to take action or improve the situation. It is a feedback loop of victimhood.

- **Nate-style Example:** Catching himself standing in the breakroom venting to a coworker for twenty minutes about upper management's poor communication. He realizes it changes absolutely nothing and drains his agency, so he cuts the complaint short and pivots the conversation to how his specific team can adapt.

- **Cole-style Example:** Traffic on the interstate comes to a dead halt due to an accident, guaranteeing he will be late to a meeting. Instead of gripping the steering wheel, swearing at the dashboard, and letting his blood pressure spike, he accepts he cannot move the cars and uses the trapped time to listen to an audiobook.

Carry-Card Line: If you can fix it, fix it. If you can't, complaining is just noise.

P10: Guard Your Core Values

Practice Rendering: Love deeply, but do not let infatuation or emotional highs compromise your core values or judgment.

What People Get Wrong: Interpreting this as a mandate to be a loveless, distant monk who never experiences joy. It actually means not letting the blinding, intoxicating rush of a new romance, lust, or even extreme passion for a brand-new hobby derail the foundational responsibilities and relationships you've already built.

- **Nate-style Example:** Feeling a massive, dopamine-fueled rush of excitement about a brand-new side hustle idea he had on a Wednesday. Despite the urge to lock himself in his office all weekend to build it, he refuses to abandon his previously promised, phone-free Saturday with his wife to chase the high.

- **Cole-style Example:** Starting to date again after his messy divorce, feeling the thrill of being wanted again, but establishing and keeping firm boundaries so he doesn't compromise his morning routine or his emotional reliability with his kids to constantly appease the new partner.

Carry-Card Line: Enjoy the fire, but don't let it burn down the house.

P11: Cultivate Adaptability

Practice Rendering: Cultivate the adaptability to work with whatever tools, conditions, or circumstances you are handed.

What People Get Wrong: They mistake this for having no standards or accepting mediocrity. You are allowed to have high-end preferences, but you cannot be *dependent* on them. If your morning routine, your workout, or your deep work shatters the second you lose your perfect conditions, your discipline is a fragile illusion.

- **Nate-style Example:** His expensive noise-canceling headphones break, the coffee machine is down, and the house is uncharacteristically loud. Instead of throwing his hands up and saying "I literally can't work in this environment," he puts in cheap foam earplugs and grinds through the spreadsheet anyway.

- **Cole-style Example:** Showing up to his hotel gym on a stressful business trip only to find a broken treadmill, a missing dumbbell, and zero space. Instead of skipping the workout because it's "suboptimal," he drops to the floor and executes a brutal, 30-minute bodyweight and burpee circuit.

Carry-Card Line: The perfect setup is a myth. Use what is in front of you.

P12: Anchor Internally, Not Externally

Practice Rendering: Find peace and focus internally, regardless of your external environment or its flaws.

What People Get Wrong: They assume this means you should be perfectly happy living in a dumpster or a toxic workplace. It actually targets the "geographical cure", the false belief that moving to a bigger house, a cooler city, or getting a nicer office will magically fix your internal chaos. If your mind is a storm, you will just bring the storm to the nicer house.

- **Nate-style Example:** Accepting that his chaotic, toy-strewn, constantly moving living room is the reality of his current season of fatherhood. Instead of constantly dreaming of escaping to a minimalist, quiet loft, he finds a way to feel grounded and present right in the middle of the mess.

- **Cole-style Example:** Being forced to move from his large, comfortable family home into a much smaller, sterile apartment after the divorce. He consciously makes the small space a place of deliberate calm and order, rather than letting it become a depressing monument to everything he lost.

Carry-Card Line: Your environment does not dictate your focus. You do.

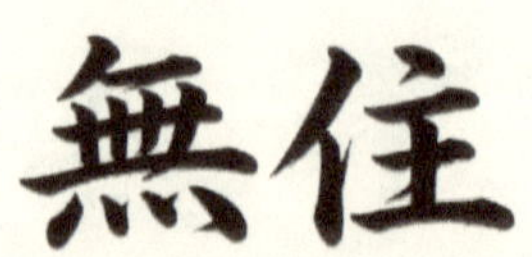

P13: Fuel Over Comfort

Practice Rendering: Treat food primarily as fuel, breaking the habit of using comfort consumption to regulate your emotions.

What People Get Wrong: They think they have to eat unseasoned chicken breast and broccoli forever, adopting a punishing diet culture. It simply means breaking the emotional dependency on "treating yourself" with sugar or heavy meals just because you had a hard day or need a distraction.

- **Nate-style Example:** Walking right past the box of 3 PM office donuts. Not because he's on a strict diet or counting macros, but because he recognizes he only wants the donut because he's highly stressed about an impending deadline, and sugar won't write the report.

- **Cole-style Example:** Traveling for work and sitting at a high-end steakhouse with clients. He skips the heavy, rich dinner and the extra drinks, ordering something clean, specifically so he doesn't wake up feeling bloated, sluggish, and behind schedule for his critical morning meetings.

Carry-Card Line: Eat for tomorrow's energy, not today's stress.

P14: Edit Your Life

Practice Rendering: Ruthlessly edit your physical and mental space, keeping only what serves your current mission.

What People Get Wrong: They confuse editing with aesthetic minimalism or self-deprivation. This rule is purely about agility and cognitive load. Carrying excess baggage, whether that is physical clutter on your desk or holding onto old, exhausting grudges, requires mental RAM. It slows down your response time to the present moment.

- **Nate-style Example:** Taking twenty minutes to clear his desk of old mail, dead hard drives, and three days' worth of coffee cups. He removes the physical, visual friction so his mind isn't distracted, allowing him to actually focus deeply on his morning anchor.

- **Cole-style Example:** Finally taking the boxes of old military gear he hasn't touched in a decade to the donation bin. He stops hoarding the physical artifacts of an old identity, freeing up space in his garage and making room for the man he is actively choosing to be right now.

Carry-Card Line: Clutter is a physical manifestation of indecision. Clear it out.

P15: Question the Default

Practice Rendering: Trust active observation over passive tradition; do what actually works, not what is merely expected.

What People Get Wrong: They think this is about being an edgy contrarian or a rebel just for the sake of making noise. It's actually about ruthless efficiency and honesty: if the "normal" way your industry, your family, or your friends operate is clearly broken or toxic, you must have the courage to discard it without hesitation.

- **Nate-style Example:** Realizing the mandatory 10 AM daily video sync is entirely useless and drains team morale. He challenges the company default, risking the annoyance of middle management to replace it with a quick async text update, winning back five hours a week for his team to do actual work.

- **Cole-style Example:** Dropping the traditional, hard-nosed "tough guy dad" approach he inherited from his own father. He observes that yelling isn't making his son more disciplined; it's just making his son sneakier and more resentful. He pivots to a new, quieter, firmer approach to parenting, regardless of how "soft" it might look to other men.

Carry-Card Line: Kill the default. Tradition is not a strategy.

P16: Master the Essentials

Practice Rendering: Master a few essential tools or skills rather than hoarding gear and superficial knowledge.

What People Get Wrong: They get caught in a modern trap called "gear acquisition syndrome," genuinely believing that buying the perfect leather notebook, downloading a new productivity app, or buying expensive gym equipment is the exact same thing as actually doing the hard work.

- **Nate-style Example:** Realizing he is using app-switching as a form of procrastination. He deletes three different complex, expensive productivity platforms from his phone and goes back to a simple, cheap pen and a legal pad to aggressively manage his daily top three tasks.

- **Cole-style Example:** Spending significantly less time scrolling through fitness forums researching new, hyper-optimal, complex workout programming, and instead just putting his head down and executing the reps on the basic, boring, brutally effective barbell lifts.

Carry-Card Line: Amateurs buy equipment. Professionals buy time through mastery.

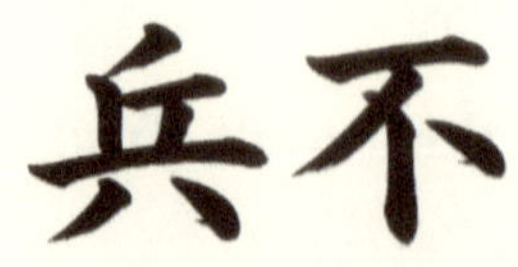

P17: Live with Urgency

Practice Rendering: Accept your mortality to live with urgency, clarity, and zero hesitation.

What People Get Wrong: They think contemplating death is morbid, depressing, or a fast track to nihilism. On the contrary, it is the ultimate prioritizing tool. If you internalize that your time is strictly limited, holding onto petty arguments, scrolling for three hours, and procrastinating your dreams suddenly become absurd.

- **Nate-style Example:** Looking at his five-year-old and getting hit with the mathematical reality that he only has so many bedtimes left while his kids are young enough to want him there. He permanently puts his phone in a drawer at 6 PM and becomes 100% present for storytime.

- **Cole-style Example:** Recognizing his father is aging rapidly. Instead of waiting for a "better time," he drives over and initiates a difficult, highly vulnerable conversation he's been putting off for a decade, knowing they are rapidly running out of time to clear the air.

Carry-Card Line: Your time is expiring right now. Act accordingly.

P18: Build Resilience, Not Hoards

Practice Rendering: Build resilience and adaptability for the future instead of anxiously hoarding resources out of fear.

What People Get Wrong: They think this means you shouldn't save for retirement, buy insurance, or plan ahead. It means not letting crippling financial anxiety or a scarcity mindset paralyze your current life, turning you rigid and isolated. True security comes from your capability to handle chaos, not just a massive bank balance.

- **Nate-style Example:** To combat his fear of industry layoffs, he doesn't just cut all his spending out of panic. He actively invests his time and a little money into learning a new, difficult skill (like coding or AI implementation) to make his brain fundamentally more adaptable and valuable in any market.

- **Cole-style Example:** Recognizing that his obsession with saving is rooted in trauma, he intentionally loosens his iron grip on the family budget to fund a spontaneous weekend trip with his kids, realizing that shared memories and connection are a far better investment right now than an extra fraction of a percent in his portfolio.

Carry-Card Line: True security is knowing you can handle whatever happens.

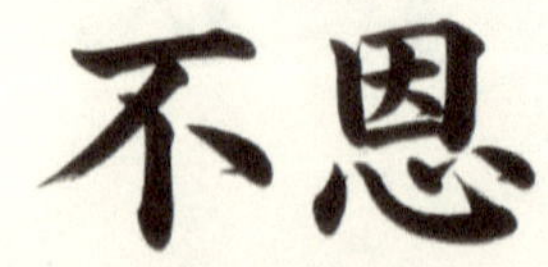

P19: Take Absolute Responsibility

Practice Rendering: Honor the unknown and respect higher powers, but take absolute, uncompromising responsibility for your own actions.

What People Get Wrong: They use luck, fate, macroeconomic conditions, or the universe as a comfortable excuse for their personal failures. Victimhood feels safe because it absolves you of the repair work. You can pray for smooth sailing or a good economy, but you still have to relentlessly row the boat yourself.

- **Nate-style Example:** A massive product launch fails entirely due to an unexpected algorithm update he couldn't possibly control. He doesn't blame the tech gods or throw a pity party; he immediately stands up in the boardroom, owns the reality of the failure, and presents the recovery plan.

- **Cole-style Example:** Acknowledging that while his divorce was highly complex and involved the actions of two people, he must take 100% ownership of his own specific character flaws, his past rigidity, and how he manages his relationship with his kids moving forward, without casting blame.

Carry-Card Line: Hope is not a strategy. You must do the work yourself.

P20: Protect Your Integrity

Practice Rendering: Protect your integrity and core character, even when it costs you comfort, status, or safety.

What People Get Wrong: They think honor is a dramatic, cinematic, battlefield concept reserved for heroes. Modern honor is incredibly boring and unglamorous. It is simply choosing to keep your word and do the right thing when it's deeply inconvenient, financially costly, and no one is watching to give you credit.

- **Nate-style Example:** Realizing a budgeting mistake he made three weeks ago just cost the company thousands of dollars. Even though he could easily bury the error or shift the blame onto a confusing software update, he chooses the sick feeling in his stomach, walks into his director's office, and owns it.

- **Cole-style Example:** Refusing to cut corners on a crucial construction safety standard to save his regional company two days of time and money, even when his direct boss quietly pressures him to look the other way and "be a team player." He holds the line.

Carry-Card Line: Your reputation is what others think. Your character is what you know.

P21: Return to the Path

Practice Rendering: Commit unconditionally to your daily practice, knowing the path is built through continuous, unglamorous return.

What People Get Wrong: They think true discipline means an unbroken streak of perfection where you never fail. This is a fragile illusion that causes people to quit on Day 4. True discipline is simply a measurement of the speed at which you return to the standard immediately after you inevitably fall short. The master fails more times than the beginner has even tried.

- **Nate-style Example:** Completely missing his morning and midday anchors because a sick kid derailed the entire schedule. Instead of declaring the day "ruined" and binge-watching TV, he grabs his notebook and does a concentrated, five-minute journal anchor in bed that night. He returns to the path before midnight.

- **Cole-style Example:** Losing his temper at a subordinate at work and shattering his stoic ideal. He doesn't spiral into self-hatred or let his ego justify the outburst. He takes a breath, walks back into the room, apologizes directly, resets his mental posture, and starts the practice over in the very next hour.

Carry-Card Line: You will stray. The discipline is in the return.

SOURCES + NOTES

Project: Dokkōdō: The Reigandō Reset **Purpose:** This document tracks the historical claims, interpretive frameworks, and translation methodology used in the manuscript to ensure historical accuracy, psychological grounding, and strict copyright compliance.

Historical Context: Musashi & The Reigandō Cave

The narrative framework of this book is grounded in the final years of Miyamoto Musashi's life. The following historical facts inform the text, specifically "Day 0" and "Day 6":

- **The Cave:** In 1643, Musashi retired to a life of asceticism in the Reigandō (霊巖洞, meaning "Spirit Rock Cave"), located on Mount Iwato near Kumamoto, Japan.

- **The Intent:** He did not go to the cave to achieve magical enlightenment, but to isolate himself, meditate, and document his life's philosophy before his impending death.

This informs our core theme: The cave isn't magic. It's just quiet, a physical representation of stripping away noise to find internal gravity.

- **The Final Work:** Musashi wrote *The Book of Five Rings* (Go Rin No Sho) in this cave. Shortly before his death in 1645, he gave away his possessions and wrote a final list of 21 precepts for his disciple, Terao Magonojō. This list was the *Dokkōdō* (The Way of Walking Alone).

- **Mortality:** The heavy emphasis on mortality and urgency in "Day 6: The Ticking Clock" is directly tied to the fact that Musashi wrote these 21 rules just days before he died of what is widely believed to be thoracic cancer.

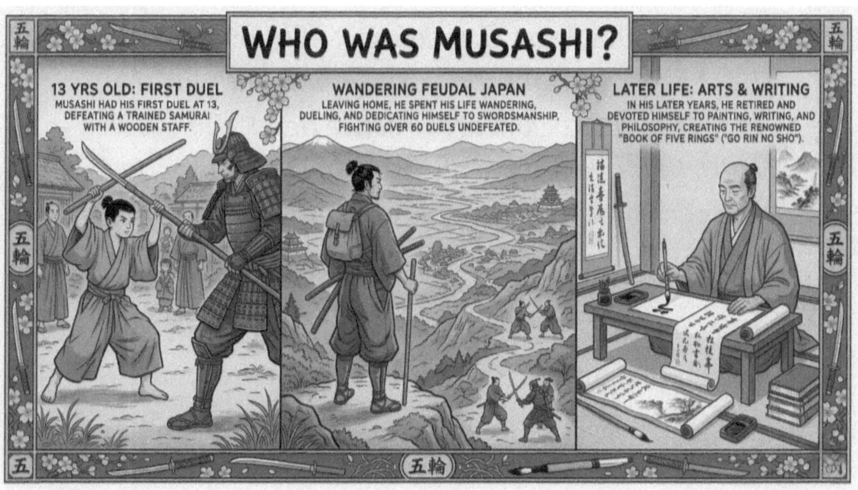

Translation Methodology & Copyright Safety

Strict Compliance: To avoid any copyright infringement of modern translations of the *Dokkōdō* (such as those by Kenji Tokitsu, William Scott Wilson, or Alexander Bennett), **no direct, literal modern translations were used in this manuscript.**

The "Practice Renderings" Framework: Instead of quoting canonical text, the manuscript utilizes a functional framework developed specifically for this book called **Practice Renderings (Plain-English).**

- These renderings distill the *intent* and *philosophical meaning* of the original 17th-century Japanese text into modern, actionable psychology.

- A mandatory disclaimer is placed before the precepts in the daily chapters: *"Disclaimer: Different translations of the historical Dokkōdō vary significantly in their wording. The rules below are Practice Renderings (Plain-English), they are unique phrasing designed strictly for modern clarity and daily application, not as canonical historical text."*

- *Note for the Author/Publisher:* If you commission a bespoke, literal translation in the future, you can safely swap it in alongside these Practice Renderings.

Interpretive & Psychological Frameworks

The avatars of Nate and Cole were designed using modern behavioral psychology models to explain *why* we fail at discipline.

- **Nate's Framework (The Flexible Path):** Grounded in modern cognitive load theory and the dopamine feedback loop. Nate exemplifies the "comfort trap." He uses digital distraction and low-friction consumption (sugar, scrolling) to manually regulate his cortisol (stress) levels.

  His path focuses on *Urge Surfing* (a real-world mindfulness and addiction-recovery technique) and removing environmental friction.

- **Cole's Framework (The Structured Path):** Grounded in the psychology of control as a trauma response. Cole uses extreme rigidity and scheduling not as a tool for freedom, but as 'emotional armor' to avoid vulnerability and the reality of impermanence. His path focuses on dismantling the Geographical Cure (the belief that external environments fix internal states) and dropping the Sunk Cost Fallacy (holding onto past mistakes or old identities).

  By utilizing these two distinct models, the book addresses the two most common ways modern people fail at discipline: chaotic lack of structure (Nate) and brittle over-structure (Cole).

Primary Bibliography

The following historical texts and translations were consulted purely to understand the historical context, chronology, and original spirit of Musashi's life and the Reigandō cave. No copyrighted text was directly reproduced.

Bennett, A. (2015). *Kendo: Culture of the Sword*. University of California Press. *(Consulted for the broader historical and cultural context of swordsmanship and asceticism in 17th-century Japan).*

Bennett, A. (2018). *The Complete Musashi: The Book of Five Rings and Other Works*. Tuttle Publishing. *(Consulted for the chronological timeline of Musashi's time in Kumamoto and his relationship with Terao Magonojō).*

Cleary, T. (1993). *The Book of Five Rings: A Classic Text on the Japanese Way of the Sword*. Shambhala Publications. *(Consulted for general philosophical themes regarding Musashi's approach to mindset and strategy).*

Lowry, T. (1985). *Autumn Lightning: The Education of an American Samurai*. Shambhala Publications. *(Consulted for the modern, grounded application of classical martial arts philosophies).*

Tokitsu, K. (2004). *Miyamoto Musashi: His Life and Writings* (S. Cowan, Trans.). Shambhala Publications. *(Consulted for the historical analysis of Musashi's final days in the Reigandō cave and the structural breakdown of the Dokkōdō).*

Wilson, W. S. (2004). *The Lone Samurai: The Life of Miyamoto Musashi*. Kodansha International. *(Consulted for biographical accuracy regarding Musashi's shift from a duelist to an ascetic).*